Editor-in-Chief and Founder:
  Lyndon H. LaRouche, Jr.
Editorial Board: *Lyndon H. LaRouche, Jr. , Helga Zepp-LaRouche, Robert Ingraham, Tony Papert, Gerald Rose, Dennis Small, Jeffrey Steinberg, William Wertz*
Co-Editors: *Robert Ingraham, Tony Papert*
Technology: *Marsha Freeman*
Books: *Katherine Notley*
Ebooks: *Richard Burden*
Graphics: *Alan Yue*
Photos: *Stuart Lewis*
Circulation Manager: *Stanley Ezrol*

INTELLIGENCE DIRECTORS
Economics: *Marcia Merry Baker, Paul Gallagher*
History: *Anton Chaitkin*
Ibero-America: *Dennis Small*
Russia and Eastern Europe: *Rachel Douglas*
United States: *Debra Freeman*

INTERNATIONAL BUREAUS
Bogotá: *Miriam Redondo*
Berlin: *Rainer Apel*
Copenhagen: *Tom Gillesberg*
Lima: *Sara Madueño*
Melbourne: *Robert Barwick*
Mexico City: *Gerardo Castilleja Chávez*
New Delhi: *Ramtanu Maitra*
Paris: *Christine Bierre*
Stockholm: *Ulf Sandmark*
United Nations, N.Y.C.: *Leni Rubinstein*
Washington, D.C.: *William Jones*
Wiesbaden: *Göran Haglund*

ON THE WEB
e-mail: eirns@larouchepub.com
www.larouchepub.com
www.executiveintelligencereview.com
www.larouchepub.com/eiw
Webmaster: *John Sigerson*
Assistant Webmaster: *George Hollis*
Editor, Arabic-language edition: *Hussein Askary*

EIR (ISSN 0273-6314) *is published weekly (50 issues), by EIR News Service, Inc., P.O. Box 17390, Washington, D.C. 20041-0390. (703) 297-8434*

European Headquarters: E.I.R. GmbH, Postfach Bahnstrasse 9a, D-65205, Wiesbaden, Germany
Tel: 49-611-73650
Homepage: http://www.eir.de
e-mail: info@eir.de
Director: Georg Neudecker

Montreal, Canada: 514-461-1557
eir@eircanada.ca

Denmark: EIR - Danmark, Sankt Knuds Vej 11, basement left, DK-1903 Frederiksberg, Denmark.
Tel.: +45 35 43 60 40, Fax: +45 35 43 87 57. e-mail: eirdk@hotmail.com.

Mexico City: EIR, Sor Juana Inés de la Cruz 242-2 Col. Agricultura C.P. 11360 Delegación M. Hidalgo, México D.F.
Tel. (5525) 5318-2301
eirmexico@gmail.com

Make a Four-Power Agreement Now

☐☐☐ Contents

www.larouchepub.com   Volume 45, Number 19, May 11, 2018

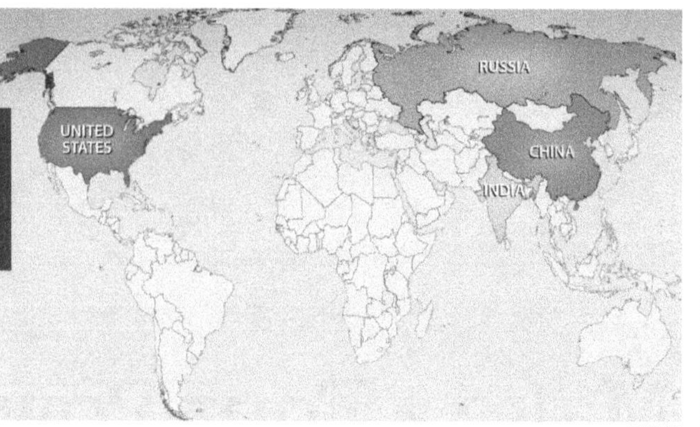

EIRNS

MAKE A FOUR-POWER AGREEMENT NOW

I. We Need It Now

ZEPP-LAROUCHE WEBCAST

The Empire Based in London Won't Give Up. They Must, and Can Be Defeated

This is the edited transcript of the May 3, 2018 Schiller Institute New Paradigm webcast, an interview with the founder of the Schiller Institutes, Helga Zepp-LaRouche. She was interviewed by Harley Schlanger. A video *of the webcast is available.*

Harley Schlanger: Hello. I'm Harley Schlanger from the Schiller Institute. Welcome to this week's Schiller Institute international webcast, featuring our President and founder, Helga Zepp-LaRouche.

There's been an incredible density of events over these last days, with the motion toward the New Paradigm and the New Silk Road, but also with a string of war provocations coming from Israel's Prime Minister, Benjamin Netanyahu, with threats to Iran. Helga, why don't we start there, because this is an extremely dangerous development, what Netanyahu did.

Helga Zepp-LaRouche: It's quite significant. Even a German politician, Norbert Röttgen, from the Christian Democratic Union (CDU), who is otherwise quite a hawk, accused Netanyahu of having committed a conscious fraud in an effort to fool the international community by claiming that Iran *is* still involved in a secret nu-

clear program. Meanwhile, the International Atomic Energy Agency (IAEA) announced that there is absolutely no truth to that claim; that it, the IAEA, has issued ten different reports showing that Iran is fully compliant with the Iran agreement on nuclear weapons, and that there is absolutely nothing new in the material presented by Netanyahu.

This was said even by a number of former security officials from Israel. So the question is, what was Netanyahu's purpose? I think it is is clearly a provocation. It's not yet entirely clear where the most recent missile attacks in Syria came from, but it's not to be excluded that they did come from Israel. Netanyahu now has a bill in the Knesset which in the first reading got an absolute majority, which would empower Netanyahu to go to war. There is some opposition in the Knesset against this, because the term "extreme circumstances" is not specified, and therefore, it's a sort of *carte blanche* because he can always declare "extreme circumstances."

This is very, very dangerous. This is obviously a power game, not really about the nations of Southwest Asia as such. Iran is the thorn in the flesh of Netanyahu, but I think the way to look at the situation is that Southwest

UN photo/J. Carrier

Prime Minister of Israel Benjamin Netanyahu talking about Iran as he addresses the UN General Assembly, Sept. 27, 2012.

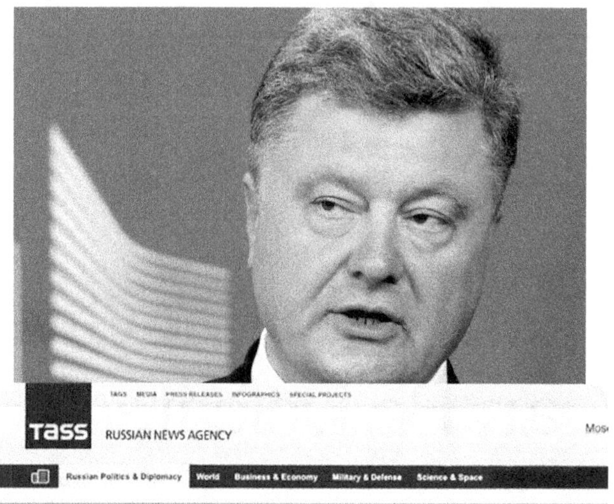

European Commission audiovisual services

President of Ukraine Petro Poroshenko announced a military solution for the "liberation" of the Donbas.

Asia is once again the theater for a proxy war, where the real issue is the confrontation against Russia and China. Rather than getting caught up in every single provocation, I encourage you, our viewers, to think about the strategic long arc of developments. I could take it back all the way to the collapse of the Soviet Union, but let's start with the election of President Trump. During the presidential election campaign he promised that he would improve the relationship with Russia. He abandoned the anti-China line that he had maintained during the election campaign soon after assuming the presidency, and instead began developing a very good relationship with Xi Jinping and China. From the standpoint of the geopolitical faction of the Western world—situated largely in the City of London and with its junior partner, Wall Street—the idea of healthy relations between the United States President and the governments of Russia and China, is a nightmare, because it absolutely eliminates the divide and conquer politics, and other geopolitical games.

Let's look at the origin of all of these developments, starting with the Russiagate hoax against Trump that is now completely out the window because *there was no*

Russiagate. The British origin and British collusion in the coup attempt against Trump became the center of attention in the Congress and other U.S. investigative committees. Then you had the Skripal affair, which, by the way, now has also completely died out; it has disappeared from the British media. Russian Foreign Ministry spokeswoman Zakharova pointed out yesterday, the Skripal affair is no longer being mentioned in the British media. When that story fell apart, you had the so-called chemical weapons attack by the Assad government, which then turned out didn't even take place—it was a complete smokescreen by the British-controlled White Helmets organization. That's fallen apart. Now, you have a supposed Iranian nuclear program, which also is a fraud. And not to be overlooked are the developments in Ukraine, where President Petro Poroshenko yesterday announced a military solution for the "liberation" of the Donbas. And there you have the same group of organizations involved which we have pinned down and published about many times in the past.

All these goings on really constitute a single long arc, aimed at the containment of Russia and China. Russia's Foreign Minister Lavrov just gave a long, very important interview to the Italian media, in which he said that every time President Trump moves to improve the U.S. relationship with Russia, the Russophobia mafia inside the United States creates a new provocation. Lavrov stressed that many of the problems of the world remain unresolved because the solutions require positive cooperation between the United States and Russia.

People have to really understand that all of these crises, while they may have some internal logic, some historical or ethnic causality, are nevertheless being played on the big chessboard in the larger game, which is the containment of Russia and China. That containment is no longer possible. We are, therefore, experiencing new tensions and very dangerous developments, almost on a daily basis.

Schlanger: That review is very useful. You can look at each individual event, but the connection is what's important. It's broader than just a regional war in the Middle East: If something happens with the Iranian nuclear agreement, that'll have an implication for what otherwise looks so positive in the Korean situation, wont it?

Xinhua/Inter-Korean Summit Press Corps

South Korean President Moon Jae-in (right) meets with Democratic People's Republic of Korea leader, Kim Jong Un, at the border village of Panmunjom for their first summit on April 27, 2018.

Zepp-LaRouche: Yes. The North Korea/South Korea process is one of the most joyful things happening right now. Some of the lesser known details are very interesting. During the meeting between Kim Jong-un and Moon Jae-in, South Korean President Moon gave a booklet and thumb drive to Kim Jong-un, detailing fully-fledged development plans for North Korea, which apparently involve, among other things, two railway lines to be built along the southern and northern coasts of North Korea, connecting both with the ancient Silk Road, but also with the Trans-Siberian Railway through Russia.

This is very positive. There has been a CIA team in North Korea for a week, inspecting various sites, and National Security Advisor John Bolton said that these are all signs of good will and that the release of three Americans being held in North Korea is possible. President Trump has let it be known that he is looking forward to meeting Kim Jong-un very soon. Kim Jong-un has expressed a desire to meet with Japanese Prime Minister Shinzo Abe, and President Moon of South Korea offered to broker such a meeting. Chinese Foreign Minister Wang Yi is in North Korea today. These are all very, very good developments, because if the Koreas achieve a peace treaty and unification under Korean sovereignty, this would a very, very important milestone for all of humanity.

But there is a danger of this being scuttled. Israeli Prime Minister Netanyahu, who wants to push the Iranian influence out of Syria—timed his statement with the May 12th deadline, which is when the United States is expected to make a decision to either extend, renegotiate, or cancel the Iranian nuclear agreement. Obviously, Netanyahu wanted to create a certain kind of hysteria, so that the United States would insist on renegotiation, which from the standpoint of the Iranians, constitutes a cancellation, and would throw the whole situation immediately into a very dangerous destabilization. It may actually lead to the desire of the Iranians to then scrap the whole deal and go back to building nuclear weapons.

Should that happen, this could threaten the North Korean situation, because, remember, Kim Jong-un began intense nuclear testing and missile testing, because he looked at the Middle East and came to the conclusion that the only way for him to prevent what happened to Saddam Hussein and Muammar al-Qaddafi from happening to him, would be for North Korea to demonstrate that it is a full-fledged nuclear power and therefore, has a defense against such things.

If Kim Jong-un came to think that even if he had an agreement with the United States, that the U.S. could throw it out on any occasion, I think this would a very, very dangerous thing. I hope that President Trump does not overlook that concern, because there is very clearly an effort to play that, to ruin the possibility of a North Korea/South Korea agreement again.

All these things hang altogether. The IAEA did say that Iran is completely in compliance with the nuclear agreement. Even Federica Mogherini, the Foreign Minister of the European Union, reiterated that the IAEA is the only institution which should be consulted concerning these questions, and should any problems arise, they should be brought to IAEA, rather than resorting to wild, independent actions, because only the IAEA is equipped to deal with such matters.

This is the field of tension in which all of this is taking place.

Schlanger: There's a kind of self-fulfilling prophecy here that the neo-conservatives play: Once you cut off negotiations and diplomatic discussion, you create what they call a "rogue state." Then they say the "rogue state" is dangerous because it doesn't adhere to principles. In fact, it is that geopolitical grouping in West that produces the fear that leads to nations backing away and developing weapons.

This is also important in the broader context. You've been pointing out the importance of the meeting between India's Prime Minister Narendra Modi and President Xi Jinping of China. This meeting has extraordinary implications, not just for those two countries, but also for another part of Southwest Asia that has been wracked by war, Afghanistan. What can you tell us about the progress on that front?

Shri Narendra Modi, Prime Minister of India (left) meeting with Xi Jinping, President of China, at an April 28, 2018 meeting in China.

Zepp-LaRouche: This may be as important as the Korean developments, because there was an effort to play India in the so-called Indo-Pacific combination—Japan, Australia, New Zealand, and India—*against* the New Silk Road and *against* China. For historical reasons, there is a strong British geopolitical influence in parts of India's establishment, which has been susceptible, and was played upon by the neo-cons and the British. That British empire faction asserts that India, being the world's largest democracy, is not interested in working with communist China but rather believes in the Western way of life, and is therefore a natural partner of the western led Indo-Pacific combination.

For a while it looked as if this manipulation would go forward. However, after the border incident at Doklam, both India and China realized how devastating it would be for the two largest countries in the world to get into some kind of a military conflict again. There was a process of rethinking in India. Most people around Modi are now moving in the direction of working with China.

That does not yet mean that India supports the New Silk Road. The issue of Pakistan is really a sticky one for India. China is building a very important China-Pakistan Economic Corridor, from China to Gwadar Port on Pakistan's Arabian Sea coast, which India completely objects to. That's why, at the Shanghai Coopera-

tion Organization (SCO) meeting, the Indian Foreign Minister did not sign the New Silk Road resolution. But India and China are now working together on the China-Nepal-India corridor, which is part of the New Silk Road.

In their "informal summit" over two days in Wuhan, China, Modi and Xi had six discussions. Remember, India and China are not only the two most populous countries—they have together 2.6 *billion* people. That's 40 percent of the entire human population of the world. They also have the longest continuous cultures, more than 5,000 years old, and have, over the course of universal history, contributed an enormous amount of knowledge, poetry, and art, and are both important creators of human civilization.

What is very exciting is that they agreed, in this context, to joint development between India and China, in war-torn Afghanistan. They will build a railroad from Iran to Afghanistan, Tajikistan, Kyrgyzstan, and China that will tie Afghanistan into the Belt and Road Initiative, which is obviously very important for Afghanistan. Several months ago, Afghanistan's President, Ashraf Ghani, had said that the only way to solve Afghanistan's problems would be as part of the New Silk Road; but it also is a way of bridging, so to speak, the India-Pakistan conflict, because there are close relations between Afghanistan and Pakistan. China has a better relationship with Pakistan than India does. If

China and India can now develop Afghanistan together, it touches on this higher level of reason, which is, as we have said from the beginning, the really essential core of the New Silk Road. You need a concept under which everybody benefits, where you have a higher level of cooperation to overcome ethnic, historical, and other conflicts.

So if India and China can work together in Afghanistan for the improvement of the situation there, this is a typical example of how the New Silk Road is also a peace initiative that can solve all kinds of problems. So I think this is a very, very good development.

Schlanger: The Pentagon has just released a report on Afghanistan, saying that after 16 years, the situation is worse—with continuous war, with both U.S. and NATO deployments. What you have just presented is the only alternative.

This brings up a very important point: In the last couple of days, we've been reviewing the role that your husband has played in bringing forward this idea of the Four Powers. His first formulation of the idea of a Four Power agreement—Russia, India, China, and the United States—was in December 2008, right after the great financial crash in September 2008. I know you've been to India, you've been to China repeatedly, you're now seeing this potential becoming real.

Zepp-LaRouche: Yes. I think it's really very good. I remember when my husband, Lyndon LaRouche, first put forward these ideas of a Four Power Agreement, everyone was full of disbelief: "How could this ever be?" But at that time he said, given that a financial oligarchy is really running so much of the world, and is using private security services that are a sort of modern mercenary force defending this financial structure, you need the four most powerful sovereign nation-states in the world to ally together to defeat it.

He emphasized that we are dealing with an empire, which is the British empire. This characterization is historically correct because, as he also developed in great detail, many times this empire—the idea of an empire with an oligarchical elite ruling over a backward mass of people—is not something new. It goes way back, even to the Roman Empire, the Byzantine Empire; then it moved to Venice, and then it became the Anglo-Dutch Empire. In a certain sense, it's like a chameleon or a slime mold: it remains the same in character, despite the fact that its colors or outward form may look different.

People nowadays often say, "Oh, the British Empire no longer exists." However, once you look at it from the standpoint of the geopolitics of the financial architecture that rules the world—which has tried in the past to keep parts of the developing sector backward and underdeveloped, and which, especially in the last 20 years, has made sure that the rich become richer, the middle class increasingly dies out, and the poor become poorer—you can see clearly that this is an empire in a modern form. It's quite powerful, it used the IMF, it used the World Bank, and kept development in the Third World down. Only after China emerged and offered cheap credit, donations, and infrastructure, did this dynamic begin to change.

As I said earlier, when Lyndon LaRouche first discussed this need for a Four Power Agreement to defeat this modern day British empire, people were full of disbelief. But as we look at the world today, we see that Russia and China have a strategic partnership which is absolutely solid, and I think will be there forever. I don't think it can ever go away. With the recent developments between China and India, India is moving closer; India already has a very good relationship to Russia. President Trump—despite the present trade negotiations—just issued a tweet saying he is looking forward to meeting President Xi Jinping in the near future and that he will always remain Xi's friend. There is also the prospect of an early meeting between Trump and Putin. We are very close to such a four-power combination that could really move the world in a completely different way, to a New Paradigm in which geopolitics stops!

Behind all of these war provocations—Russiagate, the Skripal case, the alleged chemical weapons in Syria, now Netanyahu—there is obviously an effort to keep the status quo, to prevent the emergence of China as the rising power, to keep the illusion that Russia can be contained or be regime-changed. But anyone who thinks that you can keep the status quo when the whole world is already moving in the direction of cooperation, win-win, working together—is sorely mistaken.

So I say to those in the West who are pushing these provocations, and say also to ordinary citizens, please think: Can you imagine what the future should look like, let's say, 10, 20 years from now? Either we will have World War III, or will have had it already, or, we will move into a completely new set of relations among nations, in which the common interest, or as Xi Jinping always calls it, the "shared community for the future of humanity," comes first, and after that, national interest.

It is an existential question for humanity that more and more people start to think: What should the world look like in 10 years, in 20 years? If you are of the opinion that we must develop a new phase in the evolution of mankind, in which we stop geopolitics, we stop war, and have a New Paradigm, you should become active. You should join the Schiller Institute, because we are trying to cause such a change in the thinking of the people. We need many more people to help us in this effort. I'm really appealing to you: Join the Schiller Institute and work with us, because the potential has never been so great, to move to a much, much, much more beautiful period in human history.

Schlanger: We've been talking about Lyndon LaRouche's Four Power proposal. He also has his four basic laws that address the economic crisis. People should not take their eyes off the economy! There are some new reports coming out—from former FDIC vice chairman Thomas Hoenig, and Sheila Bair, very prominent in her fight against derivatives; and now Nomi Prins has a new book out. Obviously, we ignore this financial side of things to our own detriment, because this is a crucial aspect of the strategic situation.

Zepp-LaRouche: Yes this is a very important, strategic issue. Nomi Prins's book, *Collusion: How the Central Bankers Rigged the World*—I have not read the book yet, but I have an initial report about it—describes how the quantitative easing of the central banks, to the advantage of the speculators in the last ten years, has created a situation where we are in a bubble 40 percent worse than in 2008, which could explode at any moment.

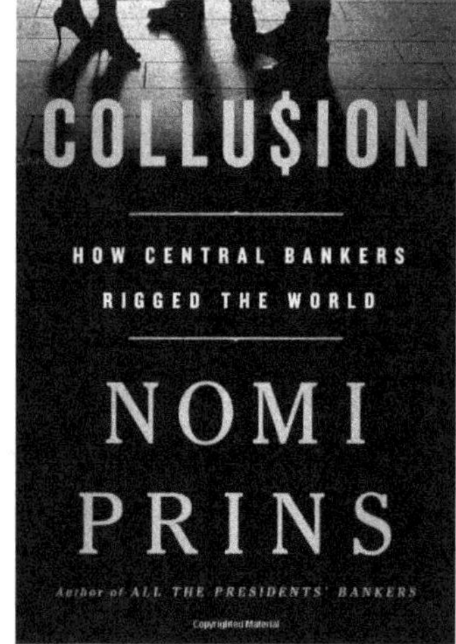

We have talked to some well-placed people in the financial community who are quite worried that what

could happen—and I think people should take this warning very seriously—if the proponents of the old, collapsing Western financial system realize that this is end-game, that they can't really prevent this from happening; that China is rising, and that the other countries are rising with China, they may *deliberately* trigger a financial crash, to pull the rug out from under President Trump, destabilize him, blame him, in order to bring the neo-cons back into power in Washington. That is one of the biggest hidden dangers.

The only way to prevent that is the immediate implementation of Glass-Steagall, but also the rest of Lyndon LaRouche's Four Laws package: a National Bank in the tradition of Alexander Hamilton; a credit system; and a crash program to increase the productivity of human labor in the production process through fusion power and cooperation in space exploration. This is necessarily part of joining the New Silk Road, joining the Belt and Road Initiative, and participating with China in the buildup of infrastructure in the United States, with joint ventures in third countries. You need the full package. By itself, reinstating Glass-Steagall is not enough. We need the return to a sound financial and economic system based on the tradition of Alexander Hamilton. Whenever that principle has been applied, as in the postwar reconstruction of Germany, you had economic miracles, and this can be replicated any time.

A financial collapse is the Damocles Sword hanging over the world, so I again urge you to join our efforts to have a global Glass-Steagall, because we don't need speculation. Let us instead put all our resources into real production, productive jobs, and education. There are so many important things to be done, that everyone will benefit. I don't think we need mega-billionaires. People should have a decent income but they shouldn't be excessively rich, and the majority of the people are poor. We really need to change that.

Schlanger: Especially when they become rich by creating things that nobody needs. To conclude, I think it's important that we provide a sense of the broader scope of what's happening around the New Silk Road. We're almost the only ones reporting on some of these things, but maybe you have something you'd like to add—the developments now in the Dominican Republic, on top of what Panama is doing, which is in our own Western Hemisphere. Peru has just moved ahead with some agreements with China, and now Portugal has

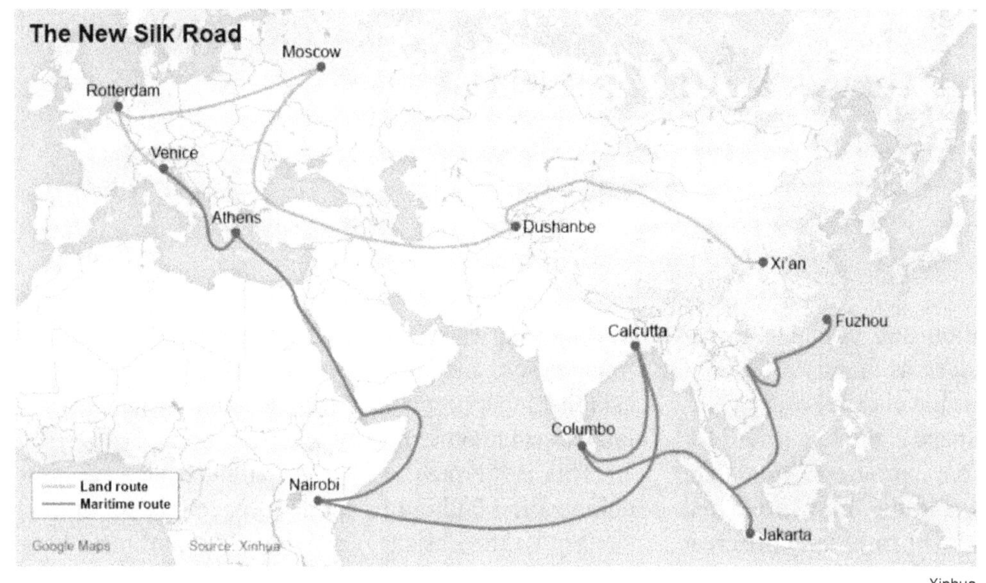

Xinhua

also, with respect to the Maritime Silk Road. The Chinese are definitely on the move.

What do you have from the U.S. Congress? The Senator from Florida—whom Donald Trump calls "little Marco Rubio"—threw a fit, saying that China is about to take over the Western Hemisphere.

Instead of embracing these initiatives, you see a certain hysteria in some quarters. Helga, I think it's important for you to emphasize the scope of this development, how it is, as you said, "unstoppable."

Zepp-LaRouche: I'm very convinced that the genie is out of the bottle, never to return. These initiatives appeal to the best inspiration and aspiration of the people. Looking at the world map, the majority of countries are already on board: That's why I think it's unstoppable. In Europe, for example, Eastern and Central European countries are working with the Silk Road, as are the Balkan countries. Italy, Spain, and Portugal all want to be hubs of development, not only for Eurasian connections, but also for the Spanish- and Portuguese-speaking countries in Asia and Africa and Latin America. Switzerland is on board, and so is Austria, where the new government has officially made a clear commitment to cooperate strategically with the New Silk Road, announcing that it wants to take leadership in Europe, to bring the European Union into connection with the Chinese New Silk Road. Even Holland and Belgium, and the Scandinavian countries, are moving, so if you look at the map, it is really the minority of countries that are not participating in some way.

That's why I'm absolutely optimistic that if you help us to spread the news, there will be a new era of civilization, not based on war, subversion, regime-change, and coups, but on the advantage of the other, in the spirit of the Peace of Westphalia. The Spirit of the Silk Road is contagious, and it will catch on: So, help us to spread this word.

Schlanger: One of the ways you can help us, is to go to the New Paradigm Schiller Institute website, where you will find a Sign Up! option (under the Contact tab) to become a member, at whatever monthly rate you can afford. We are the most important organization in the world right now, informing people about these paradigm-changing developments. We need your support! We need your involvement. So sign up, and become a part of this.

Helga, is there anything else you want to cover today?

Zepp-LaRouche: I think everyone needs to be acutely aware we are on the verge of a new hot war. Do not underestimate that danger. The situation in Ukraine is extremely dangerous. If a war breaks out between Israel and Iran, it has the potential to immediately escalate. So don't be complacent.

On the other hand, I think we have never been so close to putting all of this behind us, because once the Four Power Agreement comes into being, there is *no* problem on the planet that cannot be solved. Don't sit on the fence! Become active, and help us to turn this into a winning direction.

Schlanger: Thank you Helga, and we'll see you again next week.

Zepp-LaRouche: Yes, I hope so. See you then.

Why and How Humanity Must Return to the Moon

by Kesha Rogers

May 5—Mankind's exploration and colonization of outer space should never be seen as merely a destination or something fun to do on the cheap. Properly understood, the exploration of space is the key driver for all human scientific and economic progress. More than that, the exploration of space and the discoveries that we will make along the way, will truly unleash great creative discoveries and our divine spark of reason that distinguishes mankind from the beasts.

Our space program must again be the driving force for making America great again, as we seek to make bold new discoveries that will not only advance our nation, but will be to the betterment of all mankind. This is why it is imperative that we take a new leap in our commitment to space exploration, in immediately moving to fulfill the intention stated by President Trump to return to the Moon and establish a permanent presence. This will require a renewed national mission to develop the whole of low Earth orbit (LEO) and cis-lunar space, and fully develop and utilize the Moon, establishing a permanent presence and settlement, as a launch pad to other nearby planetary bodies.

This is the precise conception and vision of space colonization laid out by the late space pioneer and visionary Krafft Ehricke, one which has continued to be at the forefront of American statesman and economist Lyndon LaRouche's platform for space colonization. In a report written in 1986 titled, *The Science and Technologies Needed to Colonize Mars*, LaRouche wrote,

> The ordering of the leading practical goals of our nation to be consistent with, and sparked by the Moon-Mars colonization mission assignment, essentially fulfills the practical side of our obligations to prosperity's general welfare.... The Moon-Mars colonization mission illustrates the

First ever picture of the Earth rising over the Moon, seen from Apollo 10 as it orbited the Moon.

Lyndon LaRouche, speaking at a memorial conference for Krafft Ehricke in Reston, Va. June 15, 1985.

point that what the world and our nation will be, 50 years from now, will depend upon what we do, or fail to do, during each of the five decades between now and then.

It has now been thirty-two years since LaRouche wrote this report outlining the needed direction for our space program, to develop a space development platform of the Moon, cis-lunar space, and low Earth orbit, consistent with Ehricke's vision of an "open world system." LaRouche's proposal was written only five years after the first Space Shuttle, *Columbia*, rocketed into space. It was also produced two years after President Ronald Reagan *directed NASA to build an international space station "within a decade," in his January 25, 1984 State of the Union address.* In that address, President Reagan stated,

> A space station will permit quantum leaps in our research in science, communications, and in metals and lifesaving medicines which could be manufactured only in space. We want our friends to help us meet these challenges and share in their benefits. NASA will invite other countries to participate so we can strengthen peace, build prosperity, and expand freedom for all who share our goals.

Where is our space program headed today? Are we making plans for a renewed national mission shaped around a modernized Space Transportation System and permanent presence on the Moon, as an opera-

tional base for launches to other nearby planetary bodies? Will NASA take leadership again, as a driver and leader of human progress and scientific discovery? All of these questions will not be answered in this one report, but I want to begin the much needed discussion and debate.

Input from an Expert

On the anniversary of the first Shuttle flight, the flight of *Columbia*, which launched on April 12, 1981, twenty years after the first human flight into space, I had the opportunity to meet Robert F. Thompson, former Apollo Application Program Manager (later "Skylab"), and former Program Manager for the Space Transportation System (later "Shuttle"), at his home. Now 93 years old, Thompson, a key architect of NASA's post-Apollo manned spaceflight programs, recently wrote a report to President Trump's newly formed National Space Council, titled *Making America's Space Program Great Again*. Thompson joined the NASA Space Task Group in 1958. In our discussion, I was able

The launch of space shuttle Columbia on its first mission on April 12, 1981, for an Earth-orbital mission which began a new era in space transportation.

President Donald Trump, receiving a NASA flight jacket on March 21, 2017, after signing the NASA Transition Authorization Act of 2017 at the White House.

to learn much about Bob Thompson's decades of work in our Nation's manned space program, and to speak with an individual who is determined not to see all of our nation's past accomplishments squandered.

In the overview to his report, Thompson says,

> President Trump can make America's failing manned space program great again. To do so, the incoming administration must acknowledge NASA's disarray and understand how the agency squandered America's leadership in space during the post-Apollo years. NASA and the new commercial space enterprises can successfully lead the exploration and development of Earth-Lunar space and establish a permanent American settlement on the Moon by realigning their efforts along the Space Transportation System (STS) architecture that was devised following Apollo.

Thompson continues in this overview, "The Trump Administration can restore American leadership in manned spaceflight at a price that our country can afford."

Let us look at the history of post-Apollo NASA. A new era in spaceflight began on April 12, 1981, when Space Shuttle *Columbia*, on mission STS-1, soared into orbit from NASA's Kennedy Space Center, on the 20th anniversary of the first human spaceflight, the 1961 flight of Russian cosmonaut Yuri Gagarin in *Vostok 1*. *Columbia* returned to Earth on April 14, 1981, after orbiting the Earth thirty-six times in a fifty-four hour flight, landing on the dry lakebed runway at Edwards Air Force Base in California. Space Shuttle *Columbia* was commanded by astronaut John Young, and piloted by astronaut Robert Crippen. Prior to this 1981 shuttle flight, John Young had been named the chief of the Space Shuttle Branch in the Astronaut Office, in January 1973.

Astronaut Young spoke about the shuttle program in his book, *Forever Young: A Life of Adventure in Air and Space:* "Like most who were already involved in refining the shuttle concept, what I wanted was a two-stage vehicle that was totally reusable." The Shuttle itself, because it would have a cargo bay spacious enough to accommodate large modules and other materials and equipment, would become the vital transportation system that enabled the space station to be built and operated. The fleet of shuttles flew from April 1981 to July 2011.

In his report, *Making America's Space Program Great Again*, Thompson poses many vital questions, gives his assessments on where our space program has

John Young, left, and Robert Crippen, the commander and pilot of Columbia on its first mission.

Robert F. Thompson, 1980.

gone, and speaks about what is needed to restore America's Space Program to greatness. He asks,

> How did the once dominant U.S. manned space program fall so dramatically from leadership? How did NASA spend American taxpayer dollars to build the Shuttle and the Space Station only to later cede operational control and sole access to the ISS to the Russians? Why has NASA repeatedly started, then cancelled multi-billion dollar endeavours including Space Station Freedom, the Single Stage to Orbit Space Plane and Constellation? Today, the United States can no longer launch American astronauts into low earth orbit, to the International Space Station or to destinations beyond, capabilities that now only Russia and China possess. The United States' Space Shuttles, the most advanced and capable space vehicles ever built, have been decommissioned to become museum exhibits.

Thompson relays that Apollo's architecture of disposable space vehicles was totally unsuitable for a sustainable manned space program to explore cis-lunar space, or to eventually return American astronauts to the Moon, on the annual budget levels that NASA was told to expect. Thompson and his post-Apollo human space flight team got to work on evaluating three strategies to develop reusable space vehicles, to establish permanent outposts in cis-lunar space (known as, "parking regions") that were located progressively further from the Earth, and to use these "gravity-free" outposts to create a supply chain and transportation infrastructure for establishing a permanent American settlement on the Moon.

Here, I want to focus in on the section in Thompson's blueprint that he calls the "Key Elements of the Space Transportation System (STS) Architecture." What follows are excerpts taken directly from his report:

Key Elements of the STS Architecture

Reusable Space Vehicles: The airliners that we fly in today are completely re-useable, requiring only refuelling between flights and periodic maintenance. If all—or some—of a space vehicle can be recovered and re-used, then the operational costs of spaceflight can be significantly reduced.

We envisioned that the first element of the STS

Shuttle officials Aaron Cohen (center) and Robert Thompson (right), with astronaut John Young (left) during a Shuttle briefing.

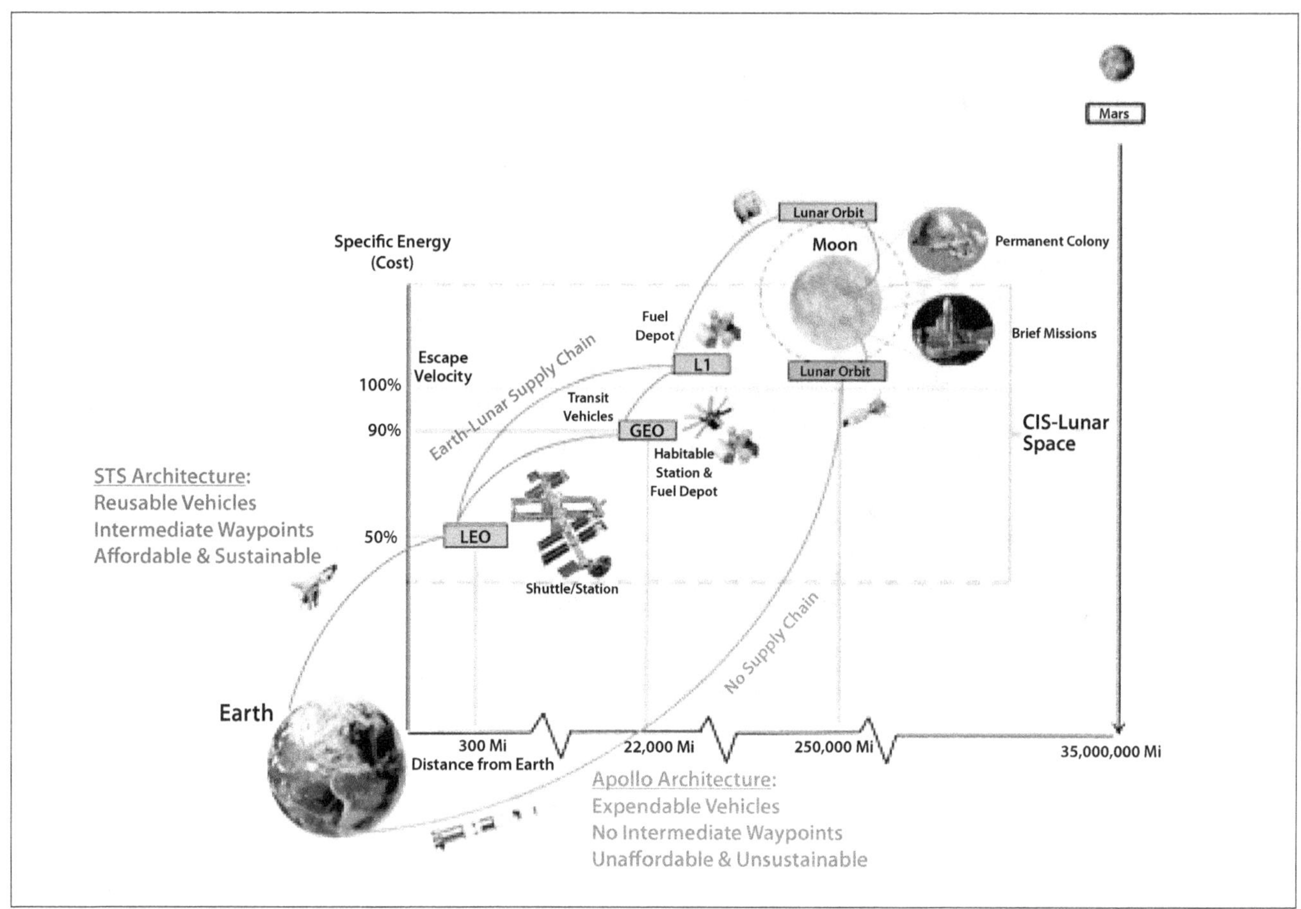

would be a reusable Shuttle to fly astronauts and cargo to and from low Earth orbit. The Shuttle would return through the atmosphere to land on a runway, a method of returning to Earth highly preferable to splashing down in the ocean to await recovery. This method required wings in our opinion. Lifting bodies were marginal.

Cis-Lunar Outposts, Waypoints & a Supply Chain to the Moon: There are locations in Cis-Lunar space where a space vehicle can remain in position with little expenditure of energy. These parking regions include low Earth orbit (LEO), geosynchronous Earth orbit (GEO), Lunar orbit and Lagrange or libration points (L1-L4) where gravitational and centripetal forces balance to allow a space vehicle or fuel depot to "hover" in position. These Cis-Lunar waypoints can be used to establish a supply chain and transportation infrastructure between the Earth and Moon.

Once flying, the Shuttle's crew/payload carrying capability would be used to assemble a permanently manned space station in LEO. Placed in a plane close to that of the lunar orbit, the space station could serve as a platform for assembling and launching a new generation of space vehicles to the Moon. We envisioned that future Lunar missions would be launched from the space station using a new generation of refuelable vehicles that were specifically designed for translunar flight, with re-entry through the Earth's atmosphere flown by the Shuttle.

To deliver the translunar vehicles to the space station for travel between the station and GEO, L1 and Lunar orbit, we envisioned a single-use Shuttle-derived cargo vehicle that could launch up to 300,000 pounds to the space station. The Shuttle-C could be cost-effectively developed by using the propulsion systems and launch infrastructure developed for the manned Shuttle.

A Permanent Moon Settlement

We envisioned that vehicles and fuel depots placed in Cis-Lunar waypoints at LEO, GEO, L1 and Lunar orbit could be used to create a supply chain and transportation infrastructure necessary to support a permanent American settlement on the Moon. Scientists and mountain climbers employ similar outposts and base camps in the exploration of Antarctica and Mt. Everest.

In contrast to the STS architecture, every Apollo mission was launched from the surface of the Earth to the Moon without establishing intermediate "gravity-free" outposts that could be used by future missions. Compared to the STS architecture, the Apollo mission profile could only support brief manned missions to the Moon and it did not provide NASA with an affordable or sustainable means for exploring Cis-Lunar space or for returning to the Moon on a realistic budget. Open ocean landing should be avoided.

As our planning concluded in the early 1970's, we thought that the new STS architecture would provide the United States with an affordable means for American astronauts to explore, utilize and develop Cis-Lunar Space for many decades in the future, culminating in a permanent American settlement on the Moon with a supply chain that stretched back to the Earth's surface.

In addition to providing a sustainable pathway for manned space exploration, each destination in Cis-Lunar space could be utilized for scientific, commercial and strategic values as shown in Table 1.

The Failure To Carry On with STS

In the section titled, "A Permanent Lunar Settlement," Thompson presents NASA's original plan under an STS architecture, for a permanent Lunar settlement. He describes the plan for STS architecture "to provide the United States with an affordable means for American astronauts to explore, utilize and develop Cis-Lunar Space for many decades in the future, culminating in a permanent American settlement on the Moon with a supply chain that stretched back to the Earth's surface." To the great detriment of the United States—and all of humanity—this plan was never carried out.

Robert Thompson, although long retired, continues to be dedicated to advancing our National Space Program and a return to Space Transportation System architecture: "For those of us who dedicated our careers to advance America's manned spaceflight program, watching the events of the past two decades unfold has been painful. Had NASA stayed with the Space Transportation System architecture, NASA's expenditures would have been more than sufficient to maintain a vigorous, ever developing American human spaceflight program."

A New Space Transportation System for the New Paradigm

The proposals of Thompson and his description of a Space Transportation System should be very seriously considered as we move to determine America's future in Space. Our commitment to the development of Cis-Lunar space and a permanent presence on the Moon is going to be of vital importance. This will also require the adoption of efficient propulsion systems, and a crash program to finally achieve controlled thermonuclear fusion technologies, a necessity that has been at the forefront of the scientific and physical-economic platform put forward by economist Lyndon LaRouche.

Table 1 – Destinations in Cis-Lunar Space for Utilization and Exploration		
Cis-Lunar Parking Regions for Waypoints & Outposts	**Utilization Value**	**Exploration Value**
Low Earth Orbit	Medical Research Microgravity Research Astronomy	Transit Station from Earth's Surface to LEO and LEO to Further Waypoints
Geosynchronous Orbit	Communications, Solar Power Generation Earth Science Continuous Earth Surveillance	Transit Station Between LEO and Translunar Destinations Fuel Depots Space Vehicle Parking
Libration Points	Earth-Lunar Communications Space Radiation Research	Fuel Depots Space Vehicle Parking
Lunar Orbit	Assembly Station	Transit Station to Lunar Surface
Lunar Surface	Permanent Manned Settlement, Astronomy	Harness Moon Resources for Oxygen and Fuel

Chris Sloan

Krafft Ehricke invented the Lunar Slide Lander as an alternative to powered descent to the lunar surface, taking advantage of the Moon's sandy and glassy soil to slow the vehicle. He created a new branch of spaceflight dynamics: harenodynamics, after the Latin word for sandy.

The development of such a space transportation system, and permanent Lunar settlement, is key to mankind's expansion throughout the Solar system. How will this be accomplished? Not by privatized, commercial space flight and "public-private partnerships" for so-called cheap tourist flights to the Lunar surface and other planetary bodies. The achievement of a permanent Lunar presence is the gateway to the development of a human economy in space. The great space pioneer, Krafft Ehricke, wrote similar concrete proposals for Lunar development. In his *Lunar Industrialization and Settlement* paper, Ehricke develops five stages of lunar development, centered on the increase of what Ehricke calls the "human sector":

The most important aspect of Lunar development lies in the human sector. It bears repeating that technological progress and environmental expansion are no substitutes for human growth and maturity, but they can help the human reach higher maturity and wisdom.

This conception of human progress must be at the forefront of the understanding of what is needed to make America's space program great again.

Ehricke's five stages of Lunar development consist of the following:

First, we examine the Moon from Earth. Second, we examine the Moon from Lunar orbit, consider the optimal site for an industrial base, and establish automated laboratories and pilot facilities on the surface. Third, we locate the best spot on the Moon for an initial industrial base, and establish it there. Fourth, from this base, we establish a larger industrial zone that can return resources to Earth while expanding across the Moon. And fifth, we expand and diversify from this initial base to create a translunar space-faring civilization.

This is the necessary future for the human species.

Kesha Rogers is an independent candidate for Congress in the 9th Congressional District in Texas.

A nuclear lunar freighter, drawn by Krafft Ehricke.

How a Nation Is Destroyed, And How It Can Save Itself

by Paul Gallagher

Sam Quinones, *Dreamland: The True Tale of America's Opiate Epidemic*
Bloomsbury Press, Paperback Edition 2016, 353 pages, $18.00.

Attorney General Jeff Sessions, after creating a Justice Department task force targeting prescription drug manufacturers and distributors of prescription opioids, was interviewed May 1 by the *Washington Post*. Sessions asked his interviewer: "Have you read *Dreamland*? For the first time, you get a glimpse of how it [the American opioid addiction epidemic] really developed."

When crime reporter Sam Quinones testified to the Senate Health, Education, Labor, and Pensions Committee on Jan. 9, 2018 on one of the greatest crimes against America in its history, he had already gone beyond the extraordinary understanding of the nation's drug addiction epidemic "glimpsed" in this book, published in 2016. He now knew that new national missions, like a "new Apollo Project" for the space program and a "new Marshall Plan" for Appalachia, were needed to lift Americans back up out of the mud of depression, personal isolation, and addiction.

But when writing *Dreamland* in 2014-15, Quinones had already grasped that

deindustrialization—the collapse of the American industrial heartland—, along with loss of belief in the goodness of government and of community of shared values, had driven this continuing mass crime, now killing 65-70,000 Americans each year and degrading the lives of millions.

Judging from the reactions of the Senators who heard his testimony, most of whom *had* read *Dreamland*, many are so struck by the details of his amazing "true tale" of U.S. mass addiction, that they choose not to hear what Quinones says about the real American values lost. These include the sense of productiveness, the value of creative participation in strengthening community and government, the ability to work through stress and pain for the sake of something better for future generations.

Quinones' true tale of the addiction epidemic is much stranger than fiction; and it can, in itself, be depressing without the idea of a national mission to reverse it. He clearly knows this.

Department of Justice

Attorney General Jeff Sessions, visiting the memorial to the victims of the opioid crisis, "Prescribed to Death," by the National Safety Council, April 12, 2018.

Anything for Money, Morphine Becomes Money

Quinones has been reporting on crime, mostly for the *Los Angeles Times*, for more than two decades; for nearly one decade around the turn of this century he lived in Mexico, found out how trafficking actually works there and lived to tell the story in two earlier books.

Only by reading this book can one take in, slowly, the literally month-by-month riveting details of 25 years of this great crime, which Quinones learned over a decade from many, many law enforcement sources, addiction experts, local elected officials and business people, physicians of many disciplines, addicts at all stages of addiction and withdrawal, heroin dealers imprisoned and at large, and others.

We can simply summarize its sequences and consequences.

• Beginning in the later 1980s, a huge campaign by some major pharmaceutical companies succeeded in corrupting the morality of large sections of the American medical community. Big Pharma rather suddenly deployed massive sales forces to doctors, employing what Wall Street has made familiar as mis-selling and fraudulent practices, on behalf of their blockbuster painkillers Oxycontin (Purdue), Vicodin (Pfizer), etc. The myth of a 100% effective but "non-addictive" analgesic—morphine after 1900, synthetic heroin from 1930 through WWII—arose again. Quack theories were published and taught, which would inspire envy in Wall Street traders and investment advisors at the peak of a bubble. Large numbers of doctors bought it.

• Big pharma also thoroughly corrupted the fields of medical training, continuing education, and consulting, entrenching the idea of "pain as the fifth vital sign" which physicians *must* measure and treat. Measuring it was a fool's errand, but treating it was deceptively easy and made virtually mandatory with the coercive complicity of the health insurers. Most doctors were swept along, and some came to operate "pill mills." The worst few even sold opioids for odd jobs, favors, or sex from patients, and/or even became addicted themselves.

• What made this moral corruption "succeed" was deindustrialization of the American manufacturing and mining heartland. It robbed the Middle West and Appalachia in the East and Southeast of steady, productive, well-paid employment—for many places, a"community keystone" employment—and relatively impoverished many in the Southwest, West, and New England as well. As towns and urban neighborhoods lost keystone work and fell apart, hard workers lost their pensions and looked to disability and workman's comp as long-lasting unemployment insurance. Formerly productive people became isolated with their aches and pains, and had little to show for them *except* disability insurance, and deep worries about their children.

• The "anything for money" moral decline was demonstrated in what was actually the leading edge of the prescription opiate epidemic in the 1990s: Seniors in towns and cities in Appalachia, with generous painkiller prescriptions for their medical conditions covered by Medicare or Medicaid, sold their extra oxycodone to high school and college students to make ends meet. In effect, grandparents dealt drugs to their grandchildren to supplement their sole income, Social Security.

• The glorification of sports at all levels—compensatory for the loss of a productive future for youth—made colleges, cities, and towns lavish money on sports facilities, and created "star" athletes who need not study for more than a barely passing grade. Professional, college, even high school teams handed out opiates free, with or without prescriptions, to their athletes for the injuries from increasingly hypercom-

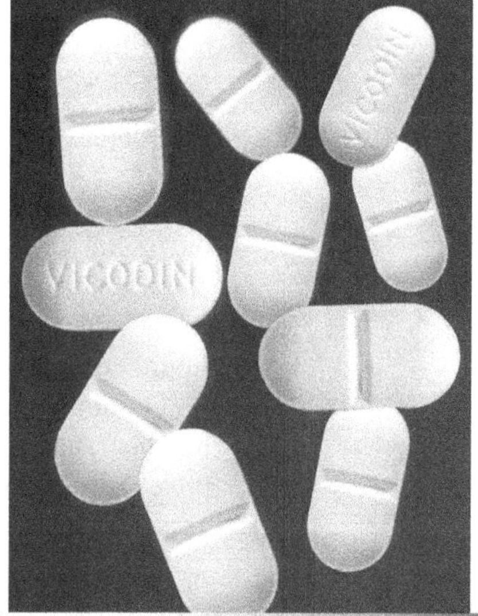

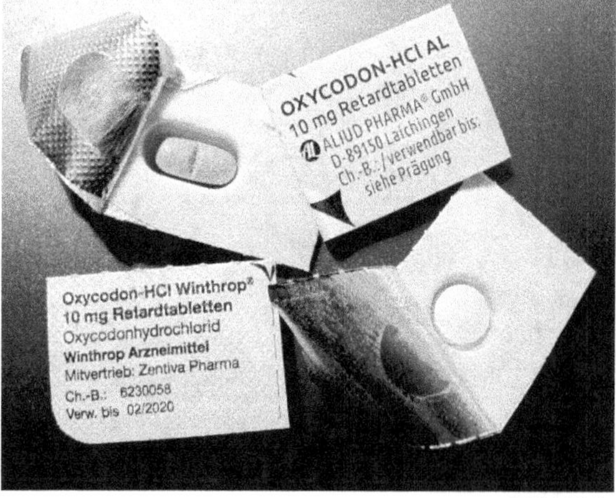

CC/GeoTrinity

Below, two tablets of the opioid Oxycodon. Above, the opioid Vicodin.

Two high school football teams taking each other on, in September 2018.

petitive sports.

By the end of the 1990s in towns and smaller cities in West Virginia, Kentucky, Ohio, Indiana, Michigan … grandparents were dealing oxycodone; quarterbacks and soccer stars were dealing it; unemployed ironworkers were dealing; popular kids in middle-class high schools were dealing. Even some doctors, besides prescribing it, were dealing.

• Other parts of the country, like the Southwest, had their own peculiar forms of spread of the habit. What all had in common was that oxycodone, by 2000 or so, had passed from being a prescription painkiller which was often abused by individuals, to an addictive drug prescribed and dealt through networks, for money, by tens of thousands, to millions.

Enter 'the Internet for Heroin'

• During the 1990s a new heroin "cartel" spread its operations from southern California eventually right across the country, to become the United States' biggest heroin-dealing force. Although these heroin dealers from the small Mexican state of Nayarit paid "protection" to the Sinaloa and Zetas cartels in order to operate—and though the big money flowed through a half-dozen extended families in Mexico—the dealers coming into the United States were unarmed youth, directed by city "cell leaders" not much older than themselves, driving tiny amounts of extremely pure and potent heroin to

addicts, like pizza delivery boys. Quinones never calls them the Nayarit cartel, but rather a new type of monster, "the Internet for heroin."

• Quinones' chronicle of the spread of this larger and larger network of 20-year-old heroin delivery boys is the most surprising part of his "true tale"; it carries an almost macabre interest for the reader. With clean-cut non-violence and addict-friendly service, avoiding gang-ridden big cities, avoiding black Americans and targeting middle-class whites, the Nayarit dealers became more proficient killers than the most violent drug gangs of New York, Baltimore, or Los Angeles.

• Finally, by the first decade of this century the leaders of "the Internet for heroin" had realized that the "chiva" they were selling, was essentially the same product as the oxycodone already being prescribed by the millions. Their version was illegal, but could be made much less expensively, while pure and potent enough to bring euphoria, or to kill. Methadone treatment centers took on particular significance for "heroin capture" of oxycodone and other opioid addicts.

The nationwide epidemic then became more and more deadly. Despite some more or less effective efforts to bring doctors, pill mills and pharma distribution companies under control; despite bigger and bigger Federal cases busting scores of heroin dealers at a time, the number of Americans dying of opiate overdoses continued to rise. And in the most recent year studied, 2016, when 65,000 died of overdoses, a full two-thirds—42,000—were killed by heroin.

What Was Destroyed

Already in writing *Dreamland*, Sam Quinones identified certain basic, bottom-up values which he thought were being wiped out by the decades of deindustrialization and privatization, replaced by forms of moral corruption.

He considers the search for an ultimate, "non-addictive" painkiller to be morally questionable and futile, and the demand to be completely free of pain as a sign of social isolation. He postulates that working through stress, and overcoming pain are a part of accomplishment, productiveness, and creativity.

He believes that working for community benefit, social and political activism, perhaps even what used to be derided as "boosterism," is also an American form of creativity. He describes community cohesion as a basic

Sam Quinones, testifying before the Senate Health, Education, Labor, and Pensions Committee, Jan. 9, 2018.

value strongly linked to places of long-lasting keystone employment, and of public recreation.

And he thinks the essential belief that government—including national government—has great potential power for the common good, has been lost in the lionization of supposed unmatched abilities of private corporations.

The question not raised in *Dreamland*, however, was: What should that potential power for common good be used to do in this crisis—even assuming renewed community activism against the ravages of addiction?

Quinones began his 10-minute Senate testimony Jan. 9 by talking about the devastation of the American heartland by free trade, globalization, privatization, and multinational corporate priorities, which have "wrought a second Gilded Age." He said the widespread addiction was "ignited by supply."

Then he proposed to the Senators:

What To Do

"View this as an opportunity to revive those regions hammered by globalization and free trade. The roots of our national epidemic of narcotic addiction lie there, while the epidemic itself, in turn, stands in the way of their revival.

"I believe American history offers us two templates for actions, from which you might take guidance and inspiration.

"The first is the Marshall Plan to rebuild Europe after World War II. The second is our space program. Each involved government and the private sector acting in concert over many years, bringing money, brains, energy, and of course long-term focus to bear. Each achieved an unalloyed good for our country; although they were both things that seemed, at first blush, far beyond our own, short-term self-interest.

"The Marshall Plan was about building up ravaged regions to allow them to function independently.... It allowed reborn countries to prosper and contribute to the world again. A Marshall Plan for American recovery might focus on rebuilding those regions that have been caught in dependence on dope, and ravaged by economic devastation, to contain the viral spread of addiction." [China's West Virginia investments irresistably come to mind.]

"Through our space program we were inspired as a people, to spend years and dollars, all to achieve something no previous generation ever thought possible. We ended up far beyond the Moon. The spillover in economic benefit, increase in knowledge, and simple human inspiration, is beyond calculation.

"It seems to me that we might profitably apply these examples—the Marshall Plan, and the space program—to regions of forgotten Americans where this [addiction] problem began. Let's do it, not because it is easy, but as JFK said, because it is hard; because that's what Americans do, and have always done, at their greatest.

"Like our space program, I believe such an effort will have to last for years to be effective, focused far beyond the immediate goal of drug addiction, and on the more profound problems of community destruction and the hollowing-out of stretches of this country."

"It offers an opportunity to reinvest in areas that need it most, a chance to inspire us as Americans again, to something great....

"Do *not* miss this opportunity. It does *not* come around often.... You will be remembered for acting, when acting was not easy to do."

In two full rounds of questioning Jan. 9, involving 18 Committee members, many with Quinones' book in front of them, and many speaking at length as Senators will, *no one* recurred to his two "big ideas."

It is up to American citizens, above all those moved by Lyndon LaRouche's movement and his "Four New Laws to Save the Nation" with which Quinones' proposals resonate, to realize them.

Solving 'Big City Malaise'—China Builds 'A Model City in Human Development'

by Mike Billington

May 4—China's capital, Beijing, an ancient city of nearly 22 million residents, suffers from many of the problems facing huge cities everywhere, including extreme air pollution and traffic congestion. Yet it is nothing like New York City, which is suffering a general breakdown crisis, with crumbling subways, many dysfunctional bridges, and roads and rails treacherous to life and limb.

But China is not waiting for Beijing to collapse before planning ahead for the next 100 to 1,000 years. Uniquely in the world today, China is addressing the problem with big—very big—measures, rather than piecemeal repairs and local reforms. China is building an entirely new metropolis south of Beijing, to be called Xiong'an, forming a triangle with Beijing and Beijing's port city, Tianjin, approximately 120 km on a side.

What has long been called the "capital region" includes Beijing, Tianjin, and Hebei Province, which surrounds the two self-directed municipalities. Known as "Jing-Jin-Ji" (the abbreviation for Hebei is "Ji"), the capital region has been the subject of multiple studies and policy reforms to relieve the pressure on Beijing, including extensive high-speed and intercity rail development; a new international airport (Beijing Daxing International Airport, to open in 2019, straddling the southern border of Beijing and Hebei Province); the most heavily used subway system in the world (and the second longest after Shanghai); and multiple regulations on industrial and auto emissions. But President Xi Jinping had bigger ideas, in keeping with his visionary Belt and Road Initiative.

In April 2017, President Xi announced that the government would direct the creation of a new city south of Beijing in Hebei, to be called Xiong'an New Area, in the tradition of the Shenzhen Special Economic Zone (launched by Deng Xiaoping in 1980) in Guangzhou Province next to Hongkong, and the Pudong New Area in Shanghai (launched in 1993).

The concept is that the region, now made up of small towns, farmland, and wetlands, will begin its transformation with a 100 square kilometer center, eventually becoming a city of 2,000 square kilometers. Most "non-core" functions of the capital will be moved to Xiong'an, including certain government divisions, offices of state-owned industries, universities, and research and development institutions. An estimated one million government workers are expected to relocate in the near term. Many of the leading private Chinese companies (including Alibaba, Baidu, Tencent, and JD.com) have already set up major centers in Xiong'an.

The plan is to limit the total population in Xiong'an to five million, while capping the population of Beijing at 23 million.

Most important, the creation from scratch of this new metropolis will facilitate the economic integration

In Beijing, a woman wears a mask to protect herself from the smog.

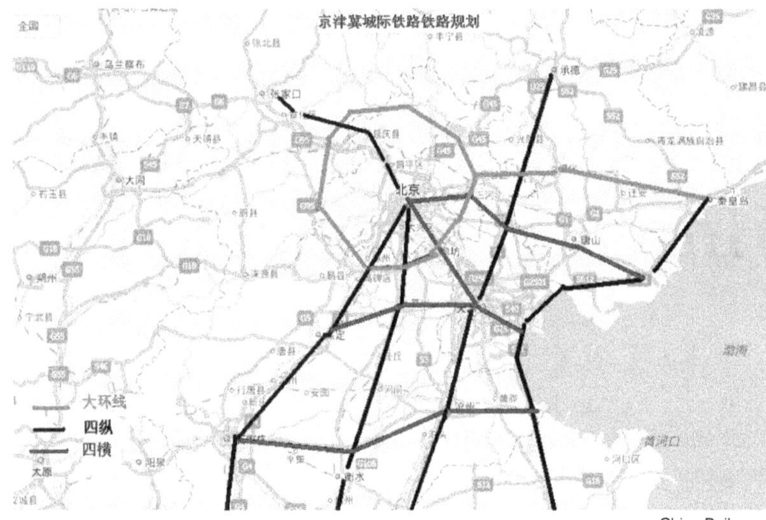

The planned railway loop around Beijing. Four vertical and four horizontal rail lines will connect the Beijing-Tianjin-Hebei capital region.

China Daily

A new metropolis south of Beijing, to be called Xiong'an New Area, will form a triangle with Beijing and Beijing's port city, Tianjin.

China Daily

of the tri-city region. An extensive network of high-speed rail and urban rail, some if it already in operation, will reduce the travel time between the three cities to between 30 minutes and one hour, and commuter time will be even less.

Official Plan Adopted

After a year of intense planning, the official blueprint for the Xiong'an New Area was adopted on April 20, 2018. Xinhua News reported that the announcement marks "a strategic decision with profound historic significance made by the Central Committee of the Communist Party of China (CPC) with Comrade Xi Jinping at the core." Xiong'an will be a "new area of 'national significance' following the Shenzhen Special Economic Zone and Shanghai Pudong New Area," according to the document, which calls it "a strategy that will have lasting importance for the millennium to come, and a significant national event." The plan calls for Xiong'an to become a modern city by 2035, and by 2050 a "significant part of the world-class Beijing-Tianjin-Hebei city cluster, effectively performing Beijing's non-capital functions and providing the Chinese solution to 'big city malaise.'"

From Polluted Wetlands to Green City

The history of the area is fascinating. In the last years of the Northern Sung Dynasty in the late 12th Century, the government was threatened with invaders from the nomadic Khitan tribes to the north. A decision

China Daily

A new metropolis south of Beijing, to be called Xiong'an New Area, will form a triangle with Beijing and Beijing's port city, Tianjin.

was made to channel water into the region to create a "natural" defense zone—a "Great Water Wall"—stretching nearly 500 km, which was "not deep enough for boats to float on, and not shallow enough for people to walk through" (see Zhang Ling, https://the-diplomat.com/2018/04/xiongan-new-area-1000-years-of-government-intervention/). While this plan eventually failed to prevent the Mongol invasions in the 13th Century, which conquered all of China, much of the region has remained a generally useless wetlands ever since, with low population density.

Baiyang Lake, the largest freshwater lake in northern China, and a major tourist attraction, sits in the center of the Xiong'an New Area. But, due to industrial waste and over-extraction of ground water, it is heavily polluted. A major aspect of the development plan is to clean up Baiyang Lake and restructure the wetlands. Many aging and heavily polluting industrial plants in the region have been shut down. Regulations to prevent land speculation—which skyrocketed following announcement of the development plan—have been implemented, with the intention that affordable housing must be available for the influx of the new workforce.

The plan includes digging out the mud in portions of the wetlands, piling the excavated mud in the northern part of Xiong'an, and creating hills and a slanted landscape, thus draining the wetlands into an enlarged Baiyang Lake. Xu Kuangdi, head of the national experts committee for the development of Jing-Jin-Ji, told the Caixin news service on June 8, 2017 that the capital city of Lin'an in the late 12th century Southern Sung Dynasty, known today as the beautiful city of Hangzhou on the West Lake (the site of the G-20 Summit in 2016), was constructed in just this way.

Tianjin's Binhai New Area

The port city Tianjin is also being modernized, including with its own "New City," called Binhai New Area, established in 2009 (there are 19 "New Areas" in China altogether, indicating central government efforts to build modern centers for development across the country). In addition to its role as the marine gateway to northern China and a growing industrial base, Tianjin is

Xinhua/Yue Yuewei

The landscape of Yujiapu Finance District at the Binhai New Area of the China (Tianjin Municipality) Pilot Free Trade Zone.

also a major tourist center, due to its rich history. The Grand Canal, begun in the 6th Century to bring grain from the south to the Beijing area, passes through Tianjin. The Port of Tianjin was destroyed by the British in the Second Opium War in 1858-60, and again in 1900 the western powers attacked Tianjin to put down the Boxer Rebellion.

According to Yang Maorang, head of the Binhai New Area, over 2,500 projects have been moved from Beijing over the past four years with an investment of over $50 billion, including a new Science Park. The city is the home of the largest number of colleges and universities in China, as well as research centers.

Infrastructure in Jing-Jin-Ji

The basic rail plan to interconnect the entire capital region was developed before the announcement of the Xiong'an New Area, but it will remain little changed. Twenty-four intercity rail lines, totalling nearly 3,500 km of track, will link all the major areas of the region by 2050. The new ring rail around Beijing will start at the new Daxing International Airport—about a third of the way between Beijing city center and Xiong'an. Four vertical and four horizontal rail lines will connect every major center in the region. The first high-speed rail connection from Beijing to Xiong'an New Area was established on July 6, 2017.

The official blueprint for the Xiong'an New Area, released April 20, concludes that Xiong'an will become "a model city in the history of human development."

South Africa Builds on Its Nuclear Success

Dr. Kelvin Kemm is chairman of the board of the government-owned South African Nuclear Energy Corporation, known as NECSA, the acronym of its former name. He is also CEO of the consultancy, Nuclear Africa, through which he has consulted not only for the government of South Africa, but other governments including Turkey and Bolivia. Kemm received his doctorate in nuclear physics from the University of KwaZulu-Natal. He was interviewed by EIR's David Cherry on April 29.

Warren Kemm

Kelvin Kemm

EIR: South Africa is the only country on the African continent that has nuclear power—the two reactors at Koeberg, in the Western Cape, produce about 5% of South Africa's electricity. But South Africa needs more of this cheap electricity to meet the needs of a growing population, while the country continues its industrialization. There have been different plans for more nuclear power plants at least since the time of Thabo Mbeki's Presidency. Dr. Kemm, what is the current plan?

Kemm: The current situation is that nuclear is still on the agenda exactly as it was; it's unchanged. There's been somewhat of a delay because of various issues—we have a new President now, as of a couple of months ago, and a new Minister of Energy. But nothing has changed with the plan to add 9,600 MW of nuclear—to the existing total from all sources of 45,000-plus MW of electric power.

However, the wind and solar people have been making a lot noise and made quite a few inroads, in that they've influenced the public thinking a lot. In doing this, they've done quite a bit of sabotage of nuclear, in the sense that they spread false stories that nuclear power will kill your children, and that there's an unsolved waste problem, and that South African workers will not be able to meet exacting nuclear standards.

In contrast, the nuclear professionals do not attack solar and wind. We say that you're not going to run electric trains across the country on solar and wind, you're not going run the gold mines; but we have no objection to solar and wind where they can work—in rural areas and in small applications, dedicated applications—which is in stark contrast to the anti-nuclear people, who condemn anything that has the word "nuclear" associated with it.

At this stage, everything is on track, but it's all been somewhat in a holding position in the public mind because of the fighting from the anti-nuclear lobby.

EIR: One of the things that they say, again and again, is that South Africa cannot afford nuclear.

Kemm: It's totally untrue. Right now, nuclear is South Africa's cheapest electricity by far. By far. It's way under the price of the wind and the solar, and below the price of coal. I am referring to the existing Koeberg Nuclear Power Station. Now some 30 years into its life, it's proven that the decision was right, and it's still got another 30 years to go; so, we've got 30 years ahead of us of cheap nuclear power.

But they don't want to look at the evidence and see that that is what will happen with the new power stations. Instead, they do spurious calculations. For example, take the cost of the new program, which is for 9600 MW of new nuclear, and that represents three new nuclear power stations to be built sequentially over a

10-year-plus period. When the total cost is quoted up front, it is quoted for the three power stations built sequentially over a decade. But the anti-nuclear lobby takes the projected cost and makes out as if the entire amount will be spent in cash once, in the first year. What is more, they've said that it will all go to a foreign country, which is completely false.

Most of the construction of a nuclear power station is not nuclear: It's pouring of concrete, it's digging foundations, it's building walls, it's putting electrical wiring inside. It's pumps, it's valves, and so on. It's only when you actually get to the reactor vessel, what's inside the reactor vessel, that you get to the nuclear part. The rest is all completely conventional civil construction, which can be done by South Africans in South Africa. We aren't going to be importing concrete from anybody, or importing welders or machinists or workers of that kind; we have all of them.

Kelvin Kemm

The Koeberg nuclear power plant, 30 km north of Cape Town, South Africa. The plant, which includes two pressurized water reactors running on enriched uranium, is rated at 1,860 MW. It is owned and operated by the state-owned electricity corporation, ESKOM.

The anti-nuclear lobby took the figure calculated by the professionals, a projected total cost of 650 billion Rand, and escalated it to 1 trillion Rand ($100 billion). And I've seen figures in the newspapers as high as 6 trillion Rand, where they say, well, there's bound to be a delay, so add some money onto this; there's bound to be this, there's bound to be that. They'll take the projected cost of the reactor and convert it to a foreign currency, as if we'll be importing concrete at British pound or euro prices, for example, which is ridiculous. They have completely distorted the story in the eyes of the public, and done calculations based on what they think the cost will be up front, using these false computations. And they come up with silly numbers, which the professionals keep saying are just plain and simply wrong.

Nuclear Fuel Is Reliably Cheap

Where nuclear really scores is in the predictability of the fuel price for so many decades into the future. Nuclear fuel occupies such a small volume. For example, in South Africa, the Koeberg Nuclear Power Sta-

tion, which has two reactors, has been running for 30 years. All of the high-level waste, which is the spent fuel, will cover half a tennis court to no higher than a man—that's the total volume of waste for 30 years—that's all. Half a tennis court, to no higher than a man. That's all it is, and that was the volume of the uranium when it was all new. So, the total amount of uranium for 50 years, for argument's sake—half a century—will fit in something like a dozen trucks.

Even if the uranium price were to go up a lot, the amount of fuel is so small that the amount of uranium in the fuel price is little: The fuel has to be fabricated with high- precision technology, so when you buy the fuel element; only a portion of that cost is for the actual uranium inside. The fuel price is highly predictable and highly stable for very many decades into the future. And that's all you have to pay for basically, other than obviously standard maintenance and so on, which is not great because you haven't got lots of dirt around a nuclear power station. It's not like a coal-fired power station with its ash and dust and flames. A nuclear power station is a very clean operation.

They have just wangled the financial figures to the point where the public mind is distorted. It's not only a South African problem, it's worldwide. I have a colleague right now who's in Vienna at the International Atomic Energy Agency (IAEA), on a nuclear costing course, and he sent me an email a couple of days ago saying that he'd been in discussion with classmates from other countries, and they all have the same problem: That the anti-nuclear lobby is distorting the minds of the public and the public is absolutely confused.

So, it is over decades now that the nuclear people have not gone to the public and explained to the public clearly; whereas the anti-nuclear extremists explain solar and wind, which are easier to explain, but they also lie about it. They completely omit to mention that there's no solar at night, for example. Time and again in our newspapers, they announce, "100 megawatts of new solar was switched on today," and they'll add, well, that's another 100 MW. But that power is only available in the daytime. And then when you say, "Well, what happens at night?" They say, "Well, we don't know, that's not our problem." And you say: "You can't have 100 MW which goes to zero at night. Then you would have to have something else, like another 100 MW of coal or nuclear, which you switch on when the Sun goes down." These sorts of things are not explained to the public, so the public is not comparing apples and apples.

EIR: Is there another country that is going ahead with nuclear and whose financing model can be used as an example of how it actually could be done in South Africa?

Kemm: Absolutely. In fact, right now, the best example is the Barakah Nuclear Power Plant in the United Arab Emirates (UAE), which is in its completion phase now and the first reactor is getting ready to supply electricity. At the beginning of this year, the UAE appointed an American team to handle all the operations and the switch-on. The Americans didn't succeed so they were fired. They were then replaced by 80 South Africans. Right now the head of reactors 1 and 2 is Darrel Aploon from Cape Town, and the head of reactors 3 and 4 is Kevin Engel, also from Cape Town. The personal advisor to the chief executive is Thegan Govender, also from South Africa. There are 80 South Africans there now, doing a very good job in all the operations and getting the reactors up and running to provide electricity according to the IAEA rules, because that's what they have to now do, not just to trip the switch. There is a whole sequence of events to go through to make sure it's legal and within the bounds of the IAEA regulations

Kelvin Kemm

The reactor pool of the SAFARI-1 reactor at Pelindaba, near Pretoria. This 20 MW, light water-cooled, beryllium reflected reactor is used by NECSA for the production of radioisotopes and for research.

and those of the World Association of Nuclear Operators (WANO), which also oversees it, the head of which is a South African based in London.

So, we know what we're doing, and the UAE reactors have been built on time and on budget, and the cost is virtually identical to the South African calculation. If you work out what it's costing them, it is virtually to the dollar of what we calculated in the beginning: So the evidence is there, that it is right.

The German Failure

EIR: What you've just said about the UAE reactors, has that ever appeared in the South African press?

Kemm: The main daily press is not reporting this. It has only appeared, a couple of times, in technical magazines. However, in the last couple of weeks, a couple of editors have spoken to me, and it is as if they are slowly starting to see the light.

We've just had a fuss over the last month, arising from what President Ramaphosa said in January—just before he was inducted as President—when he was at the World Economic Forum in Davos. In a discussion with the press, in which he was being pushed on economic issues, somebody suddenly asked the question, "What about the nuclear?" He said we have a surplus of electricity at the moment, so there's no need to rush into an expensive nuclear build. He said the word "rush," which everybody there omitted to mention in the stories they filed. Everyone reported that he said, "We don't need nuclear because we have a surplus"—which is not entirely true. We don't really have a surplus. I'll explain that in a moment.

Then a month after that, it was proposed that we spend 56 billion Rand on signing up for new wind and solar, which the Minister then did a fortnight ago. But nobody murmured a word in the newspapers about "what happened to the surplus that we had?" When they talked about the surplus for nuclear, all the newspapers were carrying a story that we had a surplus, we don't need the nuclear; so, it's been a very dishonest approach.

The claim of a surplus is also fictitious. Right now, on paper, we appear to have a bit of surplus electric power generating capacity. But what we actually have, for example, is 3,500 MW of gas turbine capacity for generating electricity. It's one of biggest gas turbine installations in the world. That was built as an emergency source that is only supposed to be used for an hour or two, in the event that you're really desperately short. That 3,500 MW stands switched off all day long, unless we get to an emergency situation, and it's horrendously expensive—way, way above the normal selling price of electricity. So that 3,500 is counted in, as part of the national electricity asset, and they count in solar and wind; but if it is night time and the wind doesn't blow, then that capacity just goes away like a wisp of smoke! And you only turn on the gas turbines if you have to, and then you really pay for it.

So, this apparent surplus is wrong. And in about a decade's time, between five and ten years, in fact, some of the older coal-fired power stations will be reaching end of life, and they should then be closed down. So we need to start the nuclear now, so when the nuclear is ready—the first reactor in half a dozen years' time—it

Former President Jacob Zuma visits NECSA in 2014. From right, NECSA CEO Phumzile Tshelane; Zuma; the then Energy Minister, Tina Joemat-Pettersson; and (pointing) Loyiso Tyabashe, Senior Manager for Nuclear New Build at ESKOM.

will come on stream as the current, old coal-fired power stations are going out. The wind and solar over the next 18 months is not going to help you in seven years' time, when the current older coal-powered stations are reaching end of life.

Again, the decisions have been made and precipitated a lot by the press. Certainly one thing that Donald Trump has brought to the world is this concept of "fake news," and it's really quite horrendous how bad it is in the case of nuclear power. Newspapers somehow, all over the world, have an instinct to attack nuclear power and never say anything good about it. Meanwhile, they are always worshipping solar and wind, as if they were a solution.

One has to point out to the press that Germany has gone into its major solar and wind campaign, while France is the country with the highest percentage of nuclear power in the world—France is 75% nuclear. And yet, the German price of electricity is twice the price of France, and Germany's carbon dioxide production is three times that of France. And yet, Germany's reason for going into solar and wind was to reduce CO_2 production, to be environmentally friendly. At the moment they are failing miserably. The newspapers never tell you that Germany has now gone to an emergency measure, building coal-fired power stations, new ones, of which the first three have been built and commissioned, because the wind and solar program is failing. That's not reported, *so this incredible distortion of the truth is really quite worrying*

COP21 Is Nonsense

EIR: What about this business of CO_2 as an environmental threat?

Kemm: Well, I don't believe it, anyway. But it certainly has become a political bargaining point at the moment. It is just a big hoax.

Some global warming is taking place, but that is a natural result of the movement of the planet, and the Solar system, and so on, for all time. If you look back more than a thousand years, you'll find there was a Medieval Warm Period, the MWP, it's very well documented in history. And at that stage, the temperatures were higher than they are now. That was followed by an event that's even better documented, the Little Ice Age, the LIA. And both of these phenomena were universal across the globe, they weren't localized. The Little Ice Age is documented, for example, in paintings that are hanging in art galleries now, of the Thames frozen over, to such a degree that people rode coaches up and down the Thames even in the 17th Century and after. And it was well known that crops failed; the cold periods were associated with misery, starvation, death, disease. The great plague in Europe happened during the Little Ice Age.

In contrast, the warm periods were healthy and full of prosperity. The crops all grew and people didn't die, and so on. So those are very well documented. And the current warming is just another one of them. Before the Medieval Warm Period was the Roman Warming, prior to that was the Minoan Warming, and the frequency is quite well established, and this is linked to the Solar cycle and the impingement of cosmic radiation on the Earth, which in turn affects cloud cover. And the amount of cloud cover only needs to change by about 10% or so for there to be a significant difference in the amount of sunlight getting through to the ground, and therefore either warming or cooling the planet.

There's a very good correlation between the level of Solar activity and climate. It was shown very clearly by Henrik Svensmark of Denmark. He did experiments on the theory and has written a very good book about it, called *The Chilling Stars* (2007) and there is a film, *The Cloud Mystery*. The book shows very clearly that there is a scientifically validated link between Solar activity and climate, which is being researched now. But the greenies don't want to accept that, because then they haven't got industry to blame. They need human beings to blame. If they've got people to blame, then they can accuse them and tax them and tell them to toe the line, so they can push them into their socialist-type agenda. That is the truth of the matter.

So the whole global warming business is false—the anthropogenic part of it is false; it's not a result of industrial carbon dioxide. In fact, we've been coming through one of the lowest CO_2 concentrations in a very long time, and there is evidence that shows clearly that high levels of CO_2 in the atmosphere are very good for plants. There is no doubt about that. And therefore, a much higher level than we've got now would increase plant growth, which means improved crops and general benefit environmentally for the planet.

We've been through a carbon dioxide starvation period for some time now, which thankfully we're coming out of. So this paranoia about CO_2 is just wrong. There is no manmade carbon dioxide problem, therefore, there is no manmade global warming problem.

But certainly the psychology of the moment is that everybody is out to lower carbon dioxide emissions, and nuclear power does that: It doesn't emit any carbon dioxide. If you have carbon dioxide reduction as one of your agenda points, and you want to toe the line for the COP21 international climate change agreement, then you should go for nuclear.

I met [French President] Emmanuel Macron about a year ago, face to face, and we had a chat about nuclear, and I said, why don't you brag more about nuclear? And he said his government should do that. I also said to him, the CO_2 thing is nonsense, COP21 is nonsense—we were just talking privately, the two of us—he said, "Interesting point." He didn't say, "yes" to that, and I noticed, when he spoke to President Trump the other day, he emphasized the COP21 agreement, because he is obviously trying to get the United States to join in, whereas I think what Trump has done is right. Trump has pulled out of COP21 and is saying, "We're not going to do this; it's not in our interest." And I think that's the right thing to do.

The Geography of Power Production

EIR: Can you give us a picture of what will happen—of course, South Africa is not an island—but let us attempt to visualize what will happen if South Africa does not go nuclear?

Kemm: South Africa *is* an electricity island, and that is something which is also very different from Europe. Look at a map of Europe—there's an Internet site where you can see a dynamic electricity map showing the flow of electricity throughout Europe. The whole of Western Europe is the same size as South Africa.

Now, I live in Pretoria. The distance from Pretoria to Cape Town is about the same as from Rome to London. In Europe, you'll find all electricity is interconnected, so there's no such thing as a "French" electricity grid, or a "German" electricity grid; there's one big pan-European grid. And it's all utterly automated, so if one country is short of electricity, it just flows in from its neighbors, and vice versa. A country like Germany—which is doing its wind and solar experiment—it's got a ring all the way around it of other supplies, one of the largest being the nuclear energy of France. Every time the German system doesn't work, the French nuclear flows in, which is often, to stop the German system from failing completely.

But South Africa is an electricity island. We don't have such neighbors. We've got a couple of electricity agreements with neighbors, but their power production is tiny. It's like the schoolteacher of a Grade 1 class, saying to all the kids, "If one of us falls down and breaks her leg, then everybody else will carry her to hospital." And they say, "Yes, teacher." Now, if any kid breaks his leg, the teacher will take him to hospital. But if the teacher breaks her leg, the children aren't going to carry the teacher to hospital.

So while you've got an agreement to help each other out, in reality, it doesn't work out that way. We've got the Southern African Electricity Power Pool, a grouping of a dozen or more Southern African countries, all agreeing to collaborate in electricity, and supply each other with electricity when they are short. But we have such minor producers on our borders that even if they had enough to supply some to South Africa in times of need, it would be like a grain of sand in comparison to normal South African consumption. So, we've got nothing outside our borders in the event we have a fail-

Nuclear Africa

International Atomic Energy Agency (IAEA) Director General Yukiya Amano addresses the Nuclear Africa conference, Pretoria, 2015. The conference is hosted annually by Dr. Kemm's consultancy.

ure. We can't just pick up the telephone to neighbors and say, "Can you help us out?" which is, in effect, what the Germans can do, and the Danes, the Belgians, and so on.

We've also got to stop looking to the First World for a solution, that "the Germans must be right." But what people don't say, is "the Germans did that, but with a major French nuclear backup sitting in the wings in case they've made a mistake." We don't have that. So we have to go nuclear.

Now, in South Africa's case, if you visualize South Africa, it is essentially a triangle standing on its apex with Cape Town at the bottom by the apex, and Pretoria up nearer to the right-hand vertex at the top. All of South Africa's coal is clustered near the right-hand vertex; it's in the northeast of the country, in Mpumalanga province and the northern parts of KwaZulu-Natal province.

Currently what's happening is, the nuclear power station down at the bottom, near Cape Town, is supplying about 50% of the electricity of the Western Cape region. But the other half is coming from the coal fields. As I said earlier, that is the equivalent of supplying London half of its electricity from Rome. When I gave a talk in London, I said, "How would you like it if half of London's electricity were coming from Rome?" They were all shocked. They said, "That would be dumb; we would never do anything that stupid. It's far too risky." But we're doing that at the moment: Half of

Dr. Kemm in discussion with NECSA CEO Phumzile Tshelane (center) and others, at Nuclear Africa 2016.

the Western Cape's electricity is coming from the coal fields, farther away than London is from Rome. That's risky, particularly when we want to double the size of the country's economy. You can't double the size of the country's economy on the basis that Cape Town is put at a greater and greater risk.

If you look at cities on the eastern seaboard, like Port Elizabeth and East London, they produce zero electricity. All of their electricity comes from the coal fields. But at the moment there's a plan to build a nuclear power station at Thyspunt, near Port Elizabeth. So we have adequate coal supplies, to supply electricity to the country from the north downwards, and we have to put the nuclear power stations around the coastline from west to east—the three capes, that's the Northern Cape, Western Cape, and Eastern Cape provinces. It's those coastlines where we need the power stations, of which five sites have currently been identified and purchased. We will use seawater as a reactor coolant. The five sites are owned by Eskom, the government-owned electricity company, for nuclear development. And for two of them, the environmental impact assessments have been finished, so the sites are ready for construction to begin and site preparation can begin immediately without deciding on the international nuclear partner.

That's what we have to do. We're not trying to displace coal with nuclear. We're trying to make sure that there's adequate electricity from the south upwards with nuclear. And the demand for electric power will not be satisfied by wind and solar. You're not going to run electric trains on wind and solar; you're not going to power the giant harbor of Durban with wind and solar power: You just aren't. And the sooner people realize the reality of that, the better.

EIR: Is coal from KwaZulu-Natal and Mpumalanga being transported all the way to the Cape, a distance of almost 900 miles?

Kemm: No. They build the power stations on top of the coal mines, so the coal-fired power stations are all clustered far in the northeast. There aren't any down at the Cape. So all of the coal-fired power stations are in the north of KwaZulu-Natal and in Mpumalanga, which represent 90%, just about, of the country's electricity production. It's like powering the whole of Western Europe, but only from Austria. [laughter] So Austria supplies electricity to London, to Rome, to Copenhagen, and so on. Now you'd look at that and say, "That's crazy. You shouldn't be doing that. It's too risky; the supply lines are too long."

So we're basically supplying the entire country from the northeast corner of the triangle, with the exception of Koeberg nuclear and then a few hydro-electric schemes and a few other schemes scattered around, which make up collectively about 10% of the nation's power—a little bit more than that. But coal is just about 90%.

So, we're not trying to displace coal, we're trying to say, leave the coal in the north, but put some balancing nuclear in the south.

Alienation from Scientific Endeavor

EIR: How many years of coal does South Africa still have, assuming population increase of what—3, 4, 5% per year?

Kemm: There is still about a century's worth of coal. There have also been significant improvements in the technology of burning coal, crushing and so on. The coal is sprayed into boilers now, finer than talcum powder. It's not like the old steam locos, where you had a fireman shoveling in blocks of coal as big as your fist, or bigger. It is all ground up and then sprayed in as fine powder. So all that technology enables you to have a very high temperature, very fast burn. Also, more

The SAFARI-1 reactor building at Pelindaba.

modern mining methods mean that you take out all of the coal, whereas in the past you left considerable coal along the walls of the mine. So there's still a lot of coal left, for a long time.

EIR: But it's also a question of what kind of society South Africa intends to become: If you stay with coal, it will be different than if you say, "No, we want a society in which there are many more scientists, many more engineers. Do people ever think about that?

Kemm: Not enough. Because the scientists and engineers worldwide have traditionally not been very good marketers. We're pleased to see people like Elon Musk at the moment, who in fact comes from Pretoria, and went to Pretoria Boys High where he finished his schooling, and he's now becoming very visible, something like Bill Gates, at being a technology interpreter and showing what you can do with modern science and modern thinking. His adventurous ideas have seen him reversing spacecraft down and re-landing them on the ground successfully, and so on.

So, he's becoming a bit of a rock star of science and technology, which is what you want. But there have been pretty few of those throughout the centuries. The average man on the street knows about medicine and the names of all the surgeons in the neighborhood that are good, and they know the names of top lawyers and so on. So their work is well under-stood by our society at large. But society doesn't know what engineers really do. And science and engineering people haven't caught up and promoted it; kids grow up with the comics, and scientists are always guys in white coats in labs with bubbling test tubes, and they all appear half-crazy, pouring stuff from one flask to the other.

Kids don't grow up seeing scientists as people who save lives and do sensible things; they usually think of the mad scientist building the bomb to blow up the neighbors. So science and technology hasn't got a good image, in the sense that it doesn't sit well with members of the public.

Radioisotope Surprises

On that note, I'd like to branch into something else, that there's a lot of nuclear technology which is not nuclear *power*. So while the extreme greens are attacking the nuclear concept, they're doing a lot of other damage. For example, South Africa is currently the second biggest supplier in the world of nuclear medicine; we're major suppliers to the United States. In Pretoria we've got the only nuclear reactor in the world that runs 24 hours a day, seven days a week, producing nuclear medicine for the world, with deliveries taking place three or four times a day, every day of the year, including weekends and public holidays. We send this nuclear medicine around the world. It is a great life-saver for cancer patients, for example, and in diagnosing other diseases.

The science is now moving into nuclear therapy, very high-precision nuclear therapy. So we've been expanding that now. We have immediate plans now under way to take nuclear medicine into centers in other African countries. We have a big thrust, and I am one of those leading that thrust. We are also building a lot more centers in South Africa, and we've been just recently been invited to build new nuclear medicine centers in Europe and in the Middle East. In other words, people consider us world authorities in doing this.

Now we are also currently looking into nuclear methods to get rid of mosquitoes because of the malaria problem. We successfully killed off tsetse flies using nuclear methods. The tsetse flies in Zanzibar were completely wiped out by nuclear methods. That improved beef production by 300% and it improved human life considerably, because people have been dying from the diseases that you get from tsetse flies.

EIR: Amazing!

Kemm: Yes. We currently use nuclear methods to reduce the fruit flies in the Cape provinces, where farmers produce fruit for export. The number of fruit flies has been reduced considerably. They won't let us attempt to wipe them out entirely, because the biologists are not quite sure whether you might need the flies in some way, so they only allow the nuclear people to kill the majority of them and then they have to stop, in case you regret it, and you have to retrace your steps.

We are also looking into nuclear methods for countering rhino poaching, for example, by putting a nuclear signal into a rhino horn that will automatically sound an alarm at a customer government's border check when it goes over the border. The details are secret. And there are certain other approaches.

We also use nuclear for nondestructive testing, for example, looking for cracks in pipes where you have high-precision welds, such as in the petrochemical industry. You put in a nuclear source and use, essentially, an X-ray type technique, but with gamma-rays, to detect if there are microscopic cracks residing in the welds, in which case you fix them, otherwise they'll fracture in due course.

So these sorts of things are being done. And there's quite a large number of them. We can also tell with nuclear techniques where an elephant lived, from its tusks. An elephant's tusks grow something like a tree, with rings. Every year the elephant's tusk has another ring, like tree rings; and depending where the elephant walks over its migratory cycle, it eats different vegetation, and the different vegetation has different nuclear signatures from its uptake of radioisotopes from the soil and atmo-

A NECSA worker in the radioisotopes laboratory at Pelindaba. NECSA operates the SAFARI-1 reactor and is responsible for promoting the understanding of nuclear science and technology. The full scope of NECSA's work is illustrated in this promotional video: https://www.youtube.com/watch?v=UxPm7hVtl1s

sphere. So if you had an elephant that moved round and round in Zimbabwe for example, and another one that walked around in South Africa, we can take those two tusks and tell that this one was a Zimbabwean elephant and this one was a South African elephant; or a Kenyan elephant, or a Namibian elephant, and so on.

At the moment there's substantial ivory poaching that's going on in numbers of African countries. Every so often, tusks turn up here and the police intercept them. And a suspect will say, "No, that tusk belonged to my great-grandfather and was passed down through the family." But if it's suspected that the tusk is from another country, we now can read from these rings where the elephant walked, because you can read the vegetation that it ate. The biologist can match that vegetation to particular places. You can also read the date of death of the elephant, so you can tell the age of the tusk. So sometimes, when somebody says, "This tusk has been an heirloom in my family for 200 years," you can say, "No, this elephant was walking around four months ago."

Sex at Sterkfontein

Another interesting case recently has to do with a world-famous paleontological skull called "Mrs. Ples," found near Johannesburg; it was a real milestone in the development of paleontology and in understanding the development of humankind. It's called "Mrs." Ples because they thought it was a female; but Professor Francis Thackeray of the University of Witwatersrand has now come to the conclusion that Mrs. Ples is actually a young male. The skull was found at a cave in a place called Sterkfontein. Thackeray's paper, "Sex at Sterkfontein," reviews the gender question for this well- preserved skull. And that was done using nuclear beams from a nuclear reactor, for the first time in the world: The paleontologists were able to look at the material between the teeth and the bone of the jaw. And so, with nuclear methods, you can read the material between the teeth and the bone, and the paleontologists can then tell you whether it was a male or a female. And they've come to the conclusion now that it's almost certainly a juvenile male and not actually a female.

EIR: Are you talking about the tissue between . . .

Kemm: Yes. The tissue between the teeth and the jawbone. And by reading that tissue, they can then come to a conclusion about the gender of the skull. And that was done here at Pelindaba, the NECSA facility in Pretoria.

There are all sorts of other nuclear processes that we carry out: We make chemicals here. It's very high precision work and very rare chemicals, and for some of them, we're the only maker—or one of two or three makers—in the world. Those chemical processes come as a spinoff of the uranium enrichment program. South Africa ran a record race towards the fabrication of nuclear weapons a number of years ago. And we then built up an arsenal of nuclear weapons. Then President F.W. de Klerk at the time announced that we had the nuclear weapons and that we planned to destroy them publicly, with IAEA supervision, which is what happened. We became the first country in the world to de-

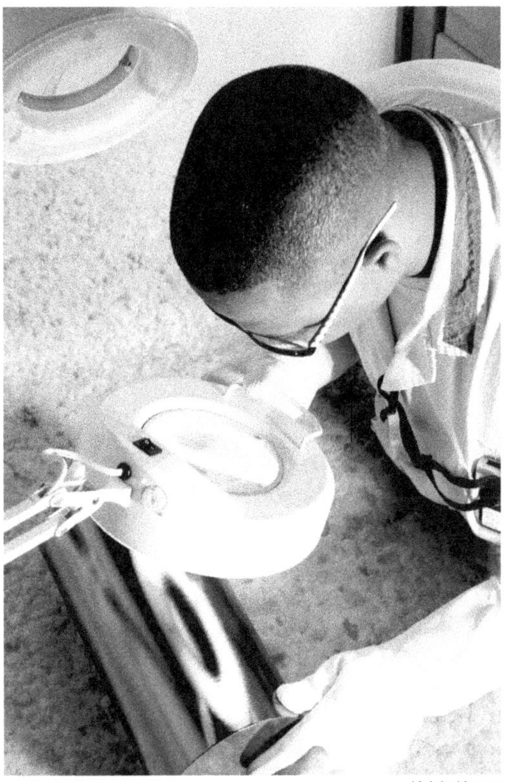

Kelvin Kemm

Worker inspecting a silicon crystal at Pelindaba. For making microchips, NECSA developed a highly efficient way to introduce phosphorus atoms uniformly throughout the silicon crystal, using a nuclear reaction between neutrons and silicon atoms.

clare that we had nuclear weapons and to then destroy them, which was done.

But that uranium enrichment program, which is the main thing in building nuclear weapons—which is what the Iranians and the Koreans and others have battled with for so many years— produced various high-precision chemicals as a spinoff. So because of that ability, we are now able to make these high-precision chemicals, which then go into as mundane a thing as toothpaste, but also into electronic chips, making the electronic chips that go into cell phones and the like. And we make numbers of other things, such as alloys for certain types of high-precision steels.

So there is a whole chemicals industry—producing and exporting these chemicals— which is a spinoff from nuclear development. So nuclear technology should be seen as highly beneficial to society, saving lives, going into commercial products. It is often overlooked that nuclear power is only one aspect of modern nuclear technology, and that it's very beneficial for mankind. So it's very unreasonable for the anti-nuclear lobby just to be anti-nuclear, full stop, as if that's the end of the argument.

EIR: I think one of the countries that's building a nuclear medicine center is Uganda.

Kemm: They're working directly with us on that. We have just recently exchanged a Memorandum of Understanding for us to work together. I sent two NECSA board members to Uganda just before Christmas, to have meetings with the senior officials there, and they came back reporting great success. And we're moving ahead now, to build the units in Uganda.

It's also of interest that Zambia has recently ordered a research reactor from the Russians, from Rosatom,

LaRouche South Africa/Tsietsi Samuel Lepele

Representatives of China's State Power Investment Corporation (SPIC) with R.P. Tsokolibane, leader of LaRouche South Africa, at the SPIC exhibit at Nuclear Africa 2016. SPIC is one of China's three nuclear power developers and operators, and is the leading nuclear power technology supplier in China

and the Russians started a nuclear university in Zambia in December 2016. The idea is that it would be a dispersed nuclear university, catering to a lot of African countries who can send people there to gain nuclear skills. And we fully support that.

Quite a lot is happening. We've also got plans in South Africa to vastly increase the nuclear medicine production here, so that we can supply even more, and over a greater area. And we're doing that in collaboration with many of these other African countries, so that, until they will be able to make the medicine themselves, we are saying, "You build the center, we will guarantee you the supplies of the medicines."

Why Africa Demands the Pebble Bed

EIR: Coming back for a moment to the nuclear power question, aren't there many countries, many governments in Africa that are very keen on moving to nuclear power?

Kemm: Yes, there are many. Last year, in 2017, I was invited to speak at the inaugural African Union Economic Platform meeting in Mauritius. One of the things I mentioned in my presentation was nuclear power for other African countries, and I was inundated with reaction.

Half-a-dozen-plus countries, now, have already spoken to us directly, asking if we can supply nuclear

power to them. Now, that is in the form of the pebble-bed modular reactor (PBMR), which South Africa developed a number of years ago. That reactor got to the point where we were ready to start constructing the first prototype, when the government of the day then put the project on ice. They didn't actually close it down, but they put it into such low gear that it eventually stumbled to an effective standstill.

However, a private company did continue with aspects of the development of the pebble-bed reactor. The pebble-bed reactor is about 5% to maybe 10% the size of the big reactors: Koeberg, for example, at the moment, is 2,000 MW; the new, big power stations that South Africa will build are going to be approximately 3,500 MW; each power station will consist of two reactors of, say, 1,500 MW each. So the pebble-bed reactor will be anywhere from 100 to 200 MW. Very small, but it's still big enough to run a smaller city—one reactor.

The huge advantage of the pebble-bed type reactors is they don't need large volumes of water for cooling, because they're gas cooled by putting helium through the core. A limitation of nuclear power up until now has been access to large volumes of water: The Russians, for example, build them on large inland lakes, and many other countries, like the United States, have tended to put them on coasts, or also on big lakes or very large rivers of guaranteed flow.

Now a lot of the landlocked African countries have not had access to water like that, because water is a reasonably scarce commodity in much of Africa. Yet many African countries are highly dependent on hydro-electric—numbers of them 100% dependent— and that's really bad news. I got quite a surprise a few years ago, when I was giving a presentation to a number of African countries, and they said to me, do you realize the difficulty with the hydro? They said that it varies depending on the rainfall. Now we've got some hydro-electric power production in South Africa, but so little that the rainfall really doesn't make a difference; if the hydro output goes down a bit, in the grand scheme of things it's not noticeable. But if hydro is 100% of your country's electricity, then it's very no-

There is great interest in nuclear power in Africa. Here, Zambian MPs visit Rosatom's Novovoronezh nuclear power plant in Russia, April 19, 2018. Patrick Matibini (fourth from left), head of delegation and chairman of the Zambian National Assembly, said, "Power is the lifeline of the economy. Most power in Zambia is produced from hydro, dependent on rainfall. And in the last years, we have had very little rainfall."

ticeable.

And at that point, I said to the people in the auditorium, "Gee whiz! If you lose 5 or 10% of your nation's output, that's serious!" And they said, "No, it's not 5 or 10%; it's 50%." The Tanzanians then took me aside and showed me some graphs. One of their power stations had lost 73% of its output! Another one, 46%. And they were averaging about 50% loss of the entire electricity output of the country, because it hadn't rained.

African dams are like saucers full of water; they tend to be pretty shallow, but with very large surface area, unlike Norwegian hydro with very steep-sided fjords. So where they've dammed the fjords, they've got a very deep head of water which is very constant, guaranteed by snow and ice run-off permanently from above, so there's no such thing as a Norwegian dam running half dry or three-quarters dry. But 50% loss of water in a South African or African dam is just common—in fact three-quarters is common. South Africa has just been going through such a drought; many of the dams are down by 75%. And when that happens, you've lost the pressure, the height of the water, to drive the turbines, and you've also lost the volume of water coming through.

So it suddenly struck me like a ton of bricks: "Golly, how can you have an African country dependent on rainfall to keep the lights on?" You just can't do that.

And numbers of them said they had no coal, oil, or gas. They said, what's next?

The anti-nuclear lobby has been going on with their hand-waving and demonstrating, to get solar and wind, but many of them have been very senseless. Hey, wait a minute—you don't get solar at night. And so hopefully the wind blows. What happens when the wind doesn't blow? Now, you've got nothing. And the green just say, well, that's the way Mother Nature designed it: Live with it.

And so, many African countries have gotten wise about it, saying, wait a minute, we're about to get suckered here into this thing. And they've realized now that the only solution they've got is to go for PBMR-type nuclear. Because with nuclear, you can stockpile fuel very easily, for a very long period of time. It's very easy to keep a year or two, or three, or four of nuclear fuel supply in a couple of bunkers, because the volume is so small; whereas you could never keep two or three years' worth of coal in a pile around a power station. Here in South Africa, we try to keep a two-week emergency supply of coal at power stations, and even that is a mountain of coal "the size of an Egyptian pyramid." And they go through that very quickly.

The Package Deal

So a number of these African countries have realized that pebble-bed reactors are the answer, and they've been coming to us, asking if we can we supply pebble-bed reactors to them? And we've been saying, yes, we can do that because we've reactivated the pebble-bed program in South Africa now, over the past year. The program at the time we left off was very close to building the first reactor. We're now in the path back to building those reactors, such that we can export the pebble-bed reactors to other African countries.

But what we would like to do is—unlike many of the colonials in years gone by,— we're aware that if

The first African Youth Nuclear Summit, in Nairobi, Kenya, March 27-30, 2017, was organized by the Kenyan Young Generation in Nuclear (KYGN) in collaboration with the African Young Generation in Nuclear (AYGN). The AYGN, founded earlier in 2017, with Gaopalelwe Santswere of NECSA (front row center, red tie) as its first president, has reached agreement with Russia's Rosatom to have its cooperation. Rosatom has an office in Johannesburg.

other African countries; where they do have them, they've currently got a regulator with a staff of three or four people to sign off the legal forms for things like the delivery of nuclear materials to certain institutions. They haven't got plans for a nuclear accident at a nuclear power station, for example, which you do need to have in place.

We could collaborate, so in the event you find a problem developing, you'd call our regulator, and we would then activate the defense force exchanges which currently do exist with many of these countries, to send, say, military aircraft with helicopters, and drop Radiation Protection Officers down to examine what's going on. That way, you overcome a lot of the startup problem, if you supply the package deal.

you sell somebody a nuclear reactor, you also need to sell them the fuel, and then you also need to be able to take the spent fuel away, so you don't give them the nuclear waste problem. You need to sell a package, like when you're buying a motor car, with—I don't know what you call it in the United States—the "freeway plan" that comes with it: You get your motor car plus the first five years of service and maintenance for free.

So the ideal would be to sell a nuclear reactor to another African country, plus the guaranteed fuel, plus the maintenance, plus guaranteed removal of the spent fuel afterwards, so they don't have to produce a national waste repository, and other things they would have to do before the International Atomic Energy Agency would sanction them getting the reactor in the first place. These are the advantages of going with a package deal, to say here's a solution, the reactor, plus the fuel, plus fuel removal, plus backup for things like emergencies.

It would mean that our nuclear regulator and their nuclear regulator would work hand-in-glove, because we've got a large, sophisticated nuclear regulator here, with about 150 staff, competent scientists, and also linkages into the defense forces—helicopters can be activated and troops, military and so on, if need be, if there's an emergency. Such regulators don't exist in

I see Africa going nuclear. There's no option. And a few governments have already said so. The President of Uganda, Yoweri Museveni, has stated that he sees Uganda becoming a nuclear-powered country, and a few other presidents have said exactly the same thing, because they see the writing is on the wall. If they want to get a much larger electricity supply, one that is reliable, they can only look toward nuclear. Other sources are not going to give it to them.

Mind Games and Fake News

EIR: Coming back for a moment to South Africa: Does business in South Africa support nuclear power?

Kemm: A lot of companies do, but a lot of them have not done so, because of this confusion. Over the last two years, there have been stories in the newspapers saying "nuclear's on," and then "nuclear's off." Now nuclear has never been off; but the anti-nuclear lobby that runs to the newspapers said, "Nuclear's stopped." For example, about a year ago now, there was a court case that the greens brought against Eskom and the Department of Energy when we had indicated that we were moving towards the beginning of the procurement cycle of the next nuclear power reactors.

The greens went to court to object to the public participation procedure, which to my mind had been done totally in accordance with the law; there was no fault there. The greens brought the court case and made a big fuss about some silly things. For example, there's also a procedure by which, if you're intending to spend a large amount of money, you notify the Treasury, so the Treasury knows the money will flow. It's not a request for money; it's just a notification that a sufficiently large amount of money will be moved, that this can have economic consequences for the country. It's called a section 34 determination. You apply for one, and the Treasury grants the section 34 by saying that we recognize that you're planning to do this. It's not a money issue.

The greens went to court and argued that the section 34 is a request to spend a lot of taxpayers' money, which it isn't. The greens fought it through the newspapers. The Department of Energy sadly didn't do its homework properly, and it sent its legal counsel to court to argue the legal points, instead of realizing they're also fighting a battle through the newspapers for the hearts and minds of the public. So, with this public circus going on, the judge ruled that everything had to be done properly and that the section 34 had to be reapplied for. That's in essence what happened. What the judge did was legally right, but he never, ever stopped the process.

But the greens then announced to the world that the nuclear program had been stopped by the judge, and many newspapers carried this erroneous story. That sowed confusion in the minds of foreigners. I had numbers of foreign countries calling me and saying, "Have you stopped the nuclear program?" and I was saying to them, "No, we haven't." We were quite happy to do exactly what the judge instructed. There was no discord between the nuclear people and what the judge said.

So that was done, but it was reported in the newspapers in such a way that numbers of businesses thought the nuclear program had been stopped. So numbers of businesses that were gearing up to be part of nuclear, then slowed down; then started again, then slowed again, and then accelerated and slowed down. Many of them said, "Forget it, we don't know whether we're coming or going." It's like training to get a gold medal at the Olympic Games, but you don't know the date of the Olympics, it would be very difficult to design a training program. For many of them, they were gearing up to start, but they didn't know what the start date was.

There have also been a number of other businesses that have seen money in solar and wind, because it's been billed as a very attractive economic proposition—which it is, when you're the foreign country supplying the solar and wind technology, and walking away with all the money—the Germans, for example.

So a few of our businesses were seduced into believing this was a real solution. But certainly, the senior businessmen are realists. They understand that if you don't get big, reliable baseload power projected well into the future, you're in trouble.

Coal Chemistry

EIR: What is the attitude of the coal-mining companies?

Kemm: We've had an interesting situation just in the past month, actually, when the coal miners suddenly swung around behind nuclear to quite a degree. The miners are interested in looking after mining jobs, and looking after the jobs of all those companies that are related to the mining industry—the people that supply all the technical equipment for mining. When the government signed the large solar and wind contract just a couple of weeks ago, the miners suddenly realized that if solar and wind are coming in, in a big way from a foreign country, that's going to reduce the dependence on coal, just as the "anti" lobby said, because the anti-nuclear lobby is also anti-coal; they're pro-wind and pro-solar, full stop.

Then the coal miners suddenly said, wait a minute, this is not a good idea. So they started to fight against the wind and solar. I had some meetings with them, and they started to realize just how bad the wind and solar is, because of their intermittent nature, and so on. We said, you're not going to run coal mines on electricity from wind and solar. If you want the coal mines to run, you need baseload electricity from coal and from nuclear. But also, what about direct heat? Others agree with me. It's well known, I believe, that South Africa was the world leader in producing petrol—gasoline—from coal. Currently about 40% of South Africa's gasoline is produced from coal; and that's the SASOL process—we're still one of the few in the world. I believe SASOL is looking into building a SASOL-process plant in the United States…

Make a Four-Power Agreement Now   37

A portion of Theewaterskloof reservoir, the largest serving Cape Town, was at 11% of capacity at the time of this photo in March 2018, showing tree stumps and sand usually submerged.

EIR: In Louisiana.

Kemm: Yes. A better future would be to use pebble-bed nuclear reactors to crack the coal, because at the moment, in a place like Secunda—a major SASOL base 80 miles from Johannesburg—of all the coal that gets trucked in there, 60% of the coal is burned to generate the heat to produce gasoline from the other 40%; but SASOL also produces things like boot polish and lipstick, and there are other fractions, even aspirin. We're the only country in the world that makes aspirin out of coal.

Coal has got a lot of valuable molecules in it, so it's a bit of a pity just to burn it. It's much more sensible to take the coal apart, molecule by molecule, so to speak, and make these waxes, like boot polish and lipsticks and aspirin and petrol and diesel and aviation fuel—there's a whole range of fuels that comes out of the different fractions of the catalytic process in the cracking of coal. I see the possibility of nuclear power turning the coal into petrol: In other words, no reduction in coal mining, so the coal miners' jobs would carry on; we just wouldn't burn it any more, we would much more clinically turn it into the valuable molecules that could be used for the building blocks for other things.

Nuclear Power for Desalination

EIR: That brings us also to the subject of using nuclear power to desalinate water cheaply.

Kemm: Yes. That is a big factor. We had a scare lately, in the last couple of months, because there has been a particularly bad drought in the Western Cape area. It even got to the point where the City of Cape Town thought it might run out of water round about now. But it hasn't; a bit of rainfall has come down. And now they're going into [southern hemisphere] winter, and that's a winter rainfall area, so they're expecting more rain to arrive. But the dams are still desperately short at the moment; some of the dams have dried up entirely—you can walk across the bottom. So the water situation is serious.

South Africa has been aware of this for centuries: We've got dams here that are designed to last for five years, for example, without any rainfall. That's unknown in Europe; in the UK, if it doesn't rain for two weeks, you get a drought, or water shortage. Here, dams are designed to sit for three or four years without rainfall.

To overcome that limitation, you'd need a much more regular water supply. How would desalination work for inland areas? Already, oil coming to South Africa from the Middle East is shipped to Durban, where it is refined to produce petrol. And that petrol is currently pumped to Johannesburg, underground, for 600 km via pipeline. It's very interesting—they put petrol into the pipeline, then they put a spacer in, and then they put diesel in, put another spacer, and put in a different grade of petrol. So you can have three or four grades of petrol or diesel and so on, travelling through the pipe, at the same time, with spacers that move through the pipe.

And that's been done for many years now, pumping petrol 600 kilometers. If you can pump petrol 600 km inland, you can do it with water very easily. So there is no reason why one can't desalinate on the coast, not only to immediately supply the Cape, for example, but also to supply locations much farther inland.

Consider what this could mean for farming. South Africa had its record maize [corn] crop ever, last year. The rainfall in the inland areas came at just the right time. But maize farming is very much like playing roulette: If you get a good rainfall year, then you get a bumper crop and you export. If you get poorer rainfall, you get a bad crop, and the country has to import maize. The unknown in the equation is the rainfall. If we could produce a lot of water, pumping it in from the coast, for example, so that you could guarantee irrigation to the maize lands, you should be able to guarantee bumper food crops every year.

So the economic advantage of desalination is not just in direct human consumption, but for an entire list of other opportunities, such as agriculture and factories, and numbers of other things that are very water dependent, which then links to the rainfall, because the rainfall is not high here.

So there is a lot of potential for nuclear power and, in fact, the pebble-bed reactors are ideally suited for desalination, because they run at very high temperatures, up to 1,000° Celsius, whereas conventional power reactors run at 200-300° Celsius. If you're running up to near 1,000° Celsius, your ability to evaporate water is much greater, so you need this greater efficiency from a small, high-temperature reactor like that. You take seawater and turn it into steam very fast and then condense the steam back into drinkable water.

EIR: Right. Is it possible that the opposition to desalination could be partly motivated by an anti-nuclear fear that if people went for desalination, it would drag in nuclear?

Kemm: Yes, there is some of that, but I think the fear of *no water* is greater. Because what we've had in the Cape, the last couple of months now, it's calmed down a little bit, but not that much; the seriousness of the water supply problem is still present now. I was in Cape Town two weeks ago and stayed in two different five-star hotels. Both hotels had removed all the bath plugs. And they just had little notices stuck on the wall saying, "Sorry you can't bathe, we haven't enough water. You can use the shower, and please keep it short." But they were actively stopping people from running full baths. There are many jokes going round about what happens when you've got no water. It's become quite a cartoonist's dream.

But it's been quite a scare. So, I think if one points out to the people that nuclear power can guarantee your water supply,— In fact, the Koeberg plant, early on, long before anybody else, started to see the drought coming. So Koeberg went into an urgent program to build an in-house desalination plant to ensure that it could supply itself.

They were three-quarters of the way through building it, when the drought was becoming very visible to the public. And then news got out that Koeberg was building a desalination plant, and people were saying, "Thank heavens, they're going to be supplying us with water." And Koeberg said, "No, we just built it for ourselves. We're going to use it, we're not giving it to anybody. It was merely to ensure that we don't run out." But they had pointed out that it can be done. And for themselves they did it in about a year or so, from scratch to design, and now, they're completely independent of the municipal water supply.

Of course, that's not the water for cooling the reactors. It's the water for running the building, the toilets, the washing of hands in the workshops, the day-to-day water consumption; some of the machinery uses freshwater, as against seawater. But it's not the vast amounts of water that's sucked out of the ocean for the reactor cooling.

EIR: But the Cape water crisis may reappear next year, isn't that true?

Kemm: It's still on, now; it's still there. But, now, at least—yes, it's highly likely to appear next year, because they're going into the rainfall season, but if the rainfall season isn't very good, if it's just normal, then it will not replenish entirely from where they stand now, because there's such a bad situation now, that it would take a particularly generous rainfall over the winter to bring them back up. But I imagine they're going to go to next year's drought season already short. So it's highly likely to come back next year.

Fusion, the Moon and Mars

EIR: Do you have thoughts about a nuclear fusion program for South Africa?

Kemm: Yes. Nuclear fusion is a dream of the whole world, and certainly as nuclear scientists, we all dream about it. South Africa ran some nuclear fusion studies quite a few years ago, and built a tokamak called the

Pebble-bed fuel ball for PBMR 1. They bounce.

Tokaloshe at Pelindaba here. The tokamak is one of the devices that look suitable for achieving sustained nuclear fusion. The Tokaloshe was worked on for a number of years and was developing a lot of the basic physics. It was never anticipated that it would actually be a power-generating plant, or anything like that. Because nobody in the world has got nuclear fusion right, yet; they've got it self-sustaining for a few moments, but there's likely to be a breakthrough at some stage. That, of course, is the dream.

So certainly, we aren't designing a nuclear fusion power plant right now, because the whole world is still waiting for the breakthrough. But everybody's got it in mind as the ideal nuclear source of power in due course. I'm sure, sooner or later, some solutions for nuclear fusion will emerge. There are not many scientific problems that stay unresolved forever.

EIR: Exactly. This is not the outlook of the pessimists!

Kemm: I also see nuclear power being the power source for the Moon and Mars, by the way—pebble-bed reactors. Because the pebble-bed fuel is about the size of a baseball, each fuel ball, whereas the fuel for a Koeberg-size power reactor is nearly a 4-meter-long metal assembly, quite a delicate metal assembly. If it was on a crane and you dropped it a couple of meters, you would wreck it. Whereas those fuel balls, you can throw them against the wall and they bounce. They're quite robust.

Fuel balls can be carried in a shopping packet [bag], basically, and they can easily be transported to the Moon and Mars in quite small containers. It's very easy to move the fuel out there. And these days, with the size of the rockets and the construction of this latest rocket of Elon Musk, the Falcon Heavy, they can lift a bus—a bus in volume and in weight.

So if it can lift a bus up into space, you can build a nuclear reactor in a number of Lego-type pods, and send it up to the Moon and drop the pods down onto the Moon's surface, or Mars, and put them together. So it's quite easy to build a whole reactor—bearing in mind it's not radioactive—until you put the fuel in it. So you have people working in the reactor, on the reactor and around the reactor, while you build it, on Mars, say. And then, come the day when you want to fuel it, you just put those fuel balls in, which could have been carried by a number of trips by then, and you can build up quite a stockpile, carrying the balls in boxes or cylinders, or however you want to pack them—as if you were transporting bread rolls or something.

EIR: Dr. Kemm, do you have a concluding thought for our readers?

Kemm: South Africa is very experienced in nuclear science and technology. This year, by the way, is the 70th anniversary of NECSA; South Africa's nuclear authority is only two years younger than the Atomic Energy Commission (AEC) of the United States. The U.S. AEC was formed in 1946; ours was formed in 1948.

The greens here often say that we're out of our depth; Africans don't understand what's going on; that we're only in the kindergarten stage, so we shouldn't be playing with the big boys; that we should stay out of this big, complicated nuclear business. But South Africa is one of the oldest nuclear countries in the world. We predate France, Japan, Russia, Germany—all of those countries. We've been in nuclear longer than they have.

January 25, 2013

NOW RETURN TO THE SUBJECT OF OUR CONSTITUTION

The Principle Involved

by Lyndon H. LaRouche, Jr.

*The single most concise summary of the documented principles on which the creation of the U.S. Federal Republic's economic design had originally depended, now remains, still today, in the contents of a book which had been titled The Political Economy of the American Revolution, that had been originally published in 1977, under the direction of editor Nancy B. Spannaus, and republished in a 1996 reprint edition, by **Executive Intelligence Review**, contents which retain their original content, up to the present date, and without regret. Also available as epub and kindle.*

*The original elements of design of the U.S. Republic's founding principles under President Washington and his Treasury Secretary Alexander Hamilton, all had depended upon the original success of the Washington Administration's design. The most crucial of the constitutional **economic** principles of the original U.S. economy, are the principles which had been provided largely by U.S. Secretary of the Treasury Alexander Hamilton. Hamilton's contributions, have never been actually outdated, as principles, since that time.*

*My own emphasis in treating **The Political Economy of the American Revolution**'s contents, as I do here, now remains essentially confined to the most relevant, second part of that publication: "Part II. The Founding Fathers," pp. 231-471, the section which contains the documentation for the founding of the still-essential, original economic principles of the U.S. Federal Government.*

All of the major errors which have occurred in the policies of our government since the time of President George Washington's terms in office, have been products

of systemic errors which had been committed by most among his successors, errors which had been introduced, later, by all but a relatively few exceptions; otherwise, most of those had been, largely misguided successors to the original Washington-Hamilton U.S. administrations. The systemic errors, whether of commission, or omission, had been products of the corrupting influences introduced from European sources, chiefly the British financial agencies, or certain French types, which had more or less controlled U.S. economic life since the end of the Presidency of George Washington.

Those foreign-directed errors which, chiefly, the British empire's financial interests had induced, had been typified by British agents associated with the "Wall Street" crowd, even back then, meaning such as Aaron Burr, and, otherwise, only typified by such followers of the traitor and British spy Burr, as Andrew Jackson and Martin Van Buren, earlier, or Theodore Roosevelt, Ku Klux Klan fanatic Woodrow Wilson, Calvin Coolidge, Harry S (no middle name) Truman, Richard Nixon, and, worst of them all, the descendants of the Prescott Bush who had backed Adolf Hitler at a crucial moment in German history. Prescott Bush's son George H.W. Bush had been what he turned out to be; but the worst of all U.S. Presidents have been that Bush's own son, the foolish George W. Bush, Jr., and the British Queen's and Tony Blair's nasty puppet, Barack Obama.

That last stated bunch of "the worst of all," are particularly notable for their complicity in suppressing the proof of the actual authorship of the original "9-11" cover-up, under the nominal administration of George W. Bush, Jr., and of the second "9-11" cover-up under

President Barack Obama of Benghazi this past September.[1] *Both of these had been actually British-Saudi operations, and, are typified by the role of the mass-murderous schemes of the wretched Tony Blair. Both of the latter set of cases had, so far, taken official actions of the characteristics of treasonous official "cover-ups" of otherwise known facts, facts which, by their very nature, have been implicitly cases of high treason against the United States.*

Otherwise, when and if those matters are now taken into account, we have, as a result, the following case of a treasonous suppression of a set of true facts which now needs to be considered, and exposed, that most urgently.

The New Matters To Be Considered

Place the treasonous suppression of the cardinal facts of the two "Nine-Eleven" cases off to one side for a moment of convenience; consider what represents the following other sets of facts:

*All of those other, later, principled elements of **a physical principle of design for a system of physical-economic science** which had been needed to be considered here, have been added from outside the original section of **The Political Economy of the American Revolution**; these had been contributed either by me, or, more frequently, in efforts shared with associates either from among my immediate associates, or others with whom the relevant measures taken were associated. That added material has been crafted during the more recent times, chiefly under my leadership, and, most frequently by my own crafting, but, as I have just*

The Political Economy of the American Revolution is "the single most concise summary of the documented principles on which the creation of the U.S. Federal Republic's economic design had originally depended," writes LaRouche.

stressed here, also with more or less large supplemental work done in immediate collaboration with sundry classes of associates from within the span of the relevant efforts at the relevant datings located somewhere within the span of 1970-2013.

In any actually competent comparison with the specifications of the policies established under the policies of President George Washington and Alexander Hamilton, they are in opposition to the ruinous incompetence of the explicitly contrary, and specific, ruinous, policies of the successive Presidencies of John Adams and Thomas Jefferson. Otherwise, James Monroe and John Quincy Adams had been among the greatest of our early Presidents, John Quincy Adams most notably. The continuing role of John Quincy Adams, both as the greatest President of that time in history, and also as that masterly patriot operating from within the House of Representatives, the master of them all of his later years, paved the way for what was implicit in Adams' association with one among his leading successors, Abraham Lincoln.[2]

In fact, it had been the economic and related policies of Abraham Lincoln (murdered by order of the highest ranks of British agencies), which had inspired the period of the direct influence of President Abraham Lincoln's heritage in shaping the great economic and strategic influence on Otto von Bismarck which had created the great economic reforms installed in Germany at the close of the 1870s, policies which coincided later with the great intentions of U.S. President William McKinley. It was only the assassination of McKinley which permitted the installation of the rabidly anglo-

---

1. Both had uttered orders banning the revelation of the evidence which had shown that the original, September 2001 "9-11" terror-attack on the United States had actually been the work of the combined British and Saudi-Arabian agencies. The same is to be said concerning President Barack Obama's frauds in the matter of "9-11" number two, in Benghazi.

2. Among John Quincy Adams' unique achievements as President, is that expressed by such facts, as that it was John Quincy Adams' Presidency which accomplished the titanic achievement of having crafted a United States united from coast to coast, and from Canada to Mexico.

As the greatest President of that time in history, and as the "masterly patriot operating from within the House of Representatives," John Quincy Adams paved the way for his leading successor, Abraham Lincoln.

other locations. The time has now come, where nothing in fact on that account need be held back.[4]

Had matters gone in the direction which I had proposed, the terrible things which have threatened both the U.S.A. and Europe now, could not have occurred as they have now done this far.

Behind, and underlying all that I have just stated, there lies a principle of history which only a tiny fraction of the leading circles of nations today have ever actually understood, at least up to this present moment. That is the situation which must now be corrected, if this planet is to outlive the atrocities which have come to reign over our United States, and also many other nations, this far.

I explain.

phile fanatic and implicit traitor Theodore Roosevelt, as his tenure enabled the participation of the U.S.A. in "World War I" conducted, for our U.S.A., under the Ku Klux Klan fanatic Woodrow Wilson.[3]

The policies of U.S. Presidents Franklin D. Roosevelt and John Fitzgerald Kennedy, and John's brother Robert, had also laid the basis for the "Strategic Defense Initiative (SDI)," a campaign which had been mustered, in part by me, from among prominent circles from such as President Ronald Reagan, and other leading public figures within the Americas and Europe, as during the interval 1977-1983 and beyond.

As a matter of fact, that assault on me and my associates launched during the middle of the nineteen-eighties and beyond, had been stated to me personally as "punishment of me and my associates" for my success in bringing the idea of the SDI to the table of not only the United States under President Ronald Reagan, but also as expressed against my important collaborators in France, Germany, Italy and certain

I. The Future as a Principle

The widespread, and wildly mistaken, but generally official belief, has been, that forecasting an economic future, in particular, must be guided by a presumed principle of mathematically statistical-forecasting methods, or the like.[5] In fact, the belief in such forecasting practices is to be seen as practically insane, when measured by its effects, and, therefore, ultimately tragic in its outcomes. The appropriately correct principle to

---

3. Theodore Roosevelt had been guided by his uncle and personal mentor, the traitor to the United States James D. Bulloch. (Cf. Anton Chaitkin, *Treason in America*, 2nd edition.)

4. As a leading political figure had it reported to me, on the occasion of my scheduled transport to prison: "You tried to make policy [referring to my keystone role in the actual launching of President Ronald Reagan's initial 1983 and continuing efforts on behalf of a Strategic Defense Initiative] without permission, and, for that, you are being punished." As is customary in such instances, a large number of those who had been my earlier associates fled in fear to join the ranks of my adversaries.

5. My first publicized forecast was that made, as an executive for a fairly large consulting firm, in the Summer of 1956, forecasting a major economic crisis to break out beginning February-March 1957. It occurred exactly on time; all visible rivals in this matter had missed the boat. A more impressive success came in the August of 1971, when every notable rival had missed the boat entirely, that internationally.

be adopted, is that mankind is provably the only known instance of a species which is intrinsically qualified with the potential for foreseeing that course of the future which foretells the probably correct choices of foresight into policy-shaping. Mankind, thus, possesses a power which is ostensibly unique to its own nature; unfortunately, few living human beings have been capable, so far, of grasping that great scientific principle which I had followed, even in the recent dates; they know that there is a terrible crisis presently, but, generally, no government has seemed to recognize the nature of the crisis publicly, still today.

The true principle of economic and related forecasting, is not to be considered as being a mere prediction of a dead-certain future state; rather, it represents the opportunity to foresee the probable consequences of a presently future choice of alternative policies for entire nations, or for mankind more widely, as now. In other words, the threat to be met as the prospective future now, or even earlier, is a matter of foreseeing choices which are yet to be presented explicitly in any presently obvious way. The worst practice of any society, is to resort to methods of statistical forecasting. In fact, the general economic doctrines of current practice, whether inside our United States, or abroad, are most fairly described as stupidity expressed as delusion.

The essence of that matter, is locatable within the realm of forecasting of those consequences which can, or could have been intelligently pre-defined in terms of comparing two or more, mutually contradictory choices of alternative futures. Most people today, especially what are usually the stubbornly incompetent statisticians, lack any competence in this matter of forecasting. The statisticians are, generally speaking, only the worst of all.

Why is that so? Try to pin-point the cause of such systemic failures of judgment among present nations generally. Why are they so stubbornly incompetent respecting issues on which the lives of most of the populations of nations presently depend?

The inherent incompetence of the methods of statistical forecasting, is to be located in the dependency, by the pretended forecaster, on a fixed, or fixed-rate scheme of future trajectories. In fact, all competent forecasting must become recognized—now urgently—as depending upon recognition of the reality, that actual human creativity is not forecastable by merely mathematical means, neither literally, nor with any significant degree of competence. All important changes in economic trends, for example, are, from a linear standpoint, discontinuous, that chiefly on account of the required standards of a truly scientific principle.

The cases of fundamental discoveries of physical principle (as by cases such as Max Planck, Albert Einstein, and the notion of the human mind presented by the collaboration of Wolfgang Köhler with Max Planck respecting the concept of the human mind) negate the misguided choice of a possibility of statistical methods of forecasting. The margin of error so indicated, is fundamental and inherent.

The Secret of the Human Mind

This distinction which I have stated here, respecting the potentials of the human mind, implicitly negates all presently conventional notions of the merely estimated ability to forecast the future. Consider some points of illustration.

There are chiefly two principal illustrations of this point: first, in the Classical methods of musical composition employed by Johann Sebastian Bach, and, secondly, such offshoots of Classical drama as Classical modes in composition of poetry and drama. As the case of Bach's two sets of preludes and fugues illustrates the point, the method of Bach in these instances, is correlated with the result of the future of that developmental process; the Bach sets of Preludes and Fugues implicitly demonstrate the proof of principle in this matter. Wilhelm Furtwängler's conception in respect to this same matter of the principled influence of the future, is typical of the relatively most advanced and also the most correct insights on this account.

However, the very same expression of principle, is native to the composition of both Classical poetic composition, and of Classical drama. There is no element of randomness, nor other "accident," in these matters.

The simple demonstration of that fact which I have just reported here, is provided by the systemic wretchedness of the music of the properly infamous failures Franz Liszt and Richard Wagner: the extension of their tendency for degeneracy, grew vastly worse over the later course of the Twentieth Century, as particularly notable in the case of the 1920s' trend of ruin in science

Did Kepler intend "vicarious hypothesis" to mean some sense of a domain of sense-perceptual objects; or, does it speak for a principle which is efficient, but not literally one of sense as perception, but only as a shadow cast as an effect?

competent physical science, are essentially interdependent processes, processes whose resonance is locatable only in the general conception of the implicit universality of a human quality of mind.

For example:

Without Classical principles of drama, the stage becomes degraded into the role of a cultural sewage-system for science and poetry alike. Without Classical artistic principles, mathematics is no longer a process of scientific discovery, but degenerates into a semblance of the frauds of Rene Descartes and Isaac Newton's worshippers. In short, the noëtic principle which is common to Classical artistic composition and creative scientific work, is left by such as them, at best, as if to rot "on the vine." The shameful case of the sheer fraud called "Isaac Newton," is typical, especially when contrasted to the discoveries of Johannes Kepler, Gottfried Leibniz, et al. The desperately needed connection for today, is best illustrated by the universality expressed in the standpoint of the personality and work of Nicholas of Cusa.

under the reign of the Bertrand Russellites. That contrast is essentially coincident in nature to those "Romantic" trends in music and poetry leading through the process of degeneration, and away from Classical artistic composition and performance, a process which has been accelerated since the policy of accelerating rates of moral and intellectual degeneracy associated with such perversions as the 1950 decrees of the Congress for Cultural Freedom.

However, similarly, the so-called "Green" cultural policy of the trans-Atlantic nations, is a systemic echo of the same moral degeneracy expressed as the Congress for Cultural Freedom. Such trends of degeneracy are at the root of the particular case of the trend of accelerating moral and intellectual degeneracy associated with trans-Atlantic cultural trends set into an accelerating motion, downward, by the assassination of President John F. Kennedy.

That is, by no means, the end of the matter at hand here.

Classical modalities in poetry, drama, and music, can not be properly separated from one another, or from a competent development process akin to truly Classical artistic composition, as, also, in physical scientific practice. Classical artistic composition and

Take, for example, the subject-matters of Classical drama and poetry: try Shakespeare, Friedrich Schiller, and Percy Bysshe Shelley, as recommended examples, as for example, as follows.

What "brings such works to a state of being 'alive'?" Compare this with the real element of genius in the discoveries by Johannes Kepler.[6] Did Kepler intend *vicarious hypothesis* to mean some sense of a domain internal to sense-perceptual objects; or, does it speak for a principle which is efficient, but not literally one of sense as perception, but only as a shadow cast as an effect? We are enabled to find a parallel for that paradox in the standard for performance of a Shakespeare drama.

We who see, and could hear, should know that the

---

6. Cf. Lyndon H. LaRouche, Jr. "Obama and the Trojan Horse!" with reference to Kepler's notions of *vicarious hypothesis*, and to the related notion of *metaphor*, **EIR**, Jan. 11, 2013 http://www.larouchepub.com/lar/2013/4002obama_trojan_horse.html.

content of actually Classical drama, such as that of Shakespeare or Friedrich Schiller, was not intended to be the visible person on stage, but an hypothetical personality worn as the merely cast image of the person acting on stage—otherwise the attempt at Classical drama were merely another silly farce.

Suddenly, then, with that thought in mind, how much of that which we might intend to experience in the performance on stage, is the real "flesh-and-blood" subject performing on stage? If you feel that what you have experienced prompts the urge to call out in recognition of the known Joe Brown on stage as being the Julius Caesar performing on stage, the drama in progress is really going very badly.

Now, follow *vicarious hypothesis*, with a try of *metaphor*. Then, reconsider the significance of the *metaphor* as if representing a *vicarious hypothesis* for that real staging which seems to exist for the intended audience as if only when being performed on a stage of the imagination, rather than merely surrogate identities for the moment, belonging to the truly gifted and insightful, *vicarious actors* performing on stage.

Take the paradoxical imagery another step forward toward actual reality. The unseen, but efficiently existing presence, as distinct from the "stand-in" which is what is presented to the senses as the vicarious performer imagined to be actually existing on stage. Such are the demeaning tricks which the folly of sense-certainty plays on whatever, and wherever the actual human personality's imagined personality might be securely snared.

Which way must it be? Which is real: the imagination that the actor performing on stage is serving as the credible actuality, or that the costumed image performing on stage is a fantasy? It is an image which has no true resemblance to that which could be presented to our mere senses from that reality which dwells on the stage of the noëtic imagination.

II. Imagination, The Secret Reality

The systemic quality of incompetence for which my argument requires a remedy to be found "on stage," can, and must be identified, but that had not been generally feasible among even leading potencies, until there had been a collapse of that authority which had been associated with the once-dominant culture represented by the outcome of Europe's "New Dark Age." The needed turnabout for change was typified by figures such as Jeanne d'Arc, the Great Ecumenical Council of Florence, France's Louis XI, and the entry of European heritages into the Americas with the achievement of the great student of Nicholas of Cusa's legacy, Christopher Columbus.

The crucially significant motive and outcome of Columbus's great achievement, reposed not merely in the fact of the landing in the region of the Caribbean, but in the actuality of the intention which Cusa's influence

---

The true principle of economic and related forecasting, is not to be considered as being a mere prediction of a dead-certain future state; rather, it represents the opportunity to foresee the probable consequences of a presently future choice of alternative policies for entire nations, or for mankind more widely, as now.

---

had brought to an escape from the mass-murder in Europe, by prompting such settlements as the Massachusetts Bay and similar settlements in the Americas, North America most notably. This was exactly as the great Nicholas of Cusa had intended in his role as, otherwise, the greatest figure in European science during his time, and so also among his actual followers, including the great, explicitly devoted follower of Cusa, Johannes Kepler.

Filippo Brunelleschi, for one, had been a high-ranking genius in the breakthroughs to modern science, both as a predecessor and contemporary of the greatest genius of that century, Nicholas of Cusa. What Cusa typifies for our consideration here, as in his **De Docta Ignorantia**, is the power of insight into domains of the real universe which are to be recognized only as beyond those meagre domains of a merely fixed quality of the powers of human sense-perception. The essential distinction to be recognized on that account, is the uniqueness of the actually human mental power which lies outside the domain of other known expressions of life as such. This distinct potency of mankind happens to coincide with the great principle of the universe which is expressed, uniquely for us today, as the power to act on the basis of the future, rather than being confined to

Filippo Brunelleschi's revolutionary "invention" of linear perspective, allowed the artist to overcome "sense-certainty," by portraying a three-dimensional universe on a two-dimensional surface. Shown (above left), Brunelleschi's perspective design for the interior of Santo Spirito church (Florence, 1440s), which is shown following construction, in the photo below. (Portrait of Brunelleschi (detail) by Masaccio, Brancacci Chapel, Florence, 1420s.)

the bestial condition of experiencing only the past and present. The image of man created in the likeness of his Creator.

I emphasize, for an essential illustration here, that the essential principle of Cusa's **De Docta Ignorantia** is to be placed precisely there, in that distinction of mankind. The most convenient demonstration of that principle in modern times to date, has been the proof supplied by Johann Sebastian Bach of the actual principle of composition presented by the design of his famous two settings of his **Preludes and Fugues**.

Hence, we must also speak of a contrary direction, down and backwards, such as the actually moral depravity of such "Romantics" as Franz Liszt and Richard Wagner, and also the cases of the even more deranged composers and performers from the Twentieth Century.

The implicit argument on this account, includes the crucial evidence embodied in the role of hearing the future in what is to be experienced as the realization of the extended future as creating the result of the present. The experimental proof, as by the greatest musical composers, is of crucial quality. Only a widespread cultivation of systemic ignorance blocks access to the essential reality which we must recognize and promote for the sake of all mankind. Fools believe, because that is their ritual. The actual evidence of a competent physical science, gives us a better precedence.

Ordinarily, commonplace opinion presumes that the present must await the virtually accidental coming of the future state of affairs. There lies the essence of the general incompetence of the conventional classrooms of respectively lower and higher gradations today.

That much said now, here, look back toward the argument of the immediately preceding chapter here.

The most customary sort of popular folly respect-

Ordinarily, commonplace opinion presumes that the present must await the virtually accidental coming of the future state of affairs. There lies the essence of the general incompetence of the conventional classrooms of respectively lower and higher gradations today.

---

ing this subject-matter, is rooted in an induced, literally bestial habit of reliance on strict observance of an alleged principle of sense-certainty. The simplest of the kinds of evidence to the contrary effect, is presented by the fact of a true discovery of a physical principle, which is (insofar as our present knowledge permits) a gift to the present from the mankind of the future. The principle of the Bach fugue, yields to us a demonstration of the same principle of the future source of what must emerge as presently discovered future human achievements, the which is intrinsic to the implications of Nicholas of Cusa's **De Docta Ignorantia**.

Once the individual human mind has been lifted above primitive notions of the meaning of experiences, we are most forcefully persuaded to the effect, that the advance of human culture from the stone-age to physical chemistry, to use of nuclear power, to thermonuclear fusion, and the matter-antimatter principle, show us the existence of a higher order of power of existence than science had presumed earlier. This distinction of the potentiality of human powers of reason, places mankind apart from all lower forms of life. These powers, which we tend to associate only with freshly minted discoveries, have demonstrably existed as potentials of this universe earlier. Indeed, all properly defined notions of scientific and related discoveries have precisely that quality of distinctively human potentialities for the future.

The principal errors of assumption which had tended the most to confuse even most educated persons today, have reposed in the intellectually brutish opinion respecting the subject of the future. Yet, in fact, in the matter of qualitative advances in the relative energy-flux density of physical-science progress, matters are seen differently. We are properly impelled to seek out our possession of the human power to craft the future which already lies pregnant within the domain of the present.

The consequence of a refusal "to face up to" the evidence of such a challenge, leads toward the absurd presumption, that it is the mechanisms of mere sense-perception, which place absolute limits on the powers for physical-science progress. The actually greatest scientists, as since Nicholas of Cusa, have recognized the nature of the intrinsic incompetence of the believers in an absolute value of what was always merely sense-impression. "Who protests against this?" "How could we have been so duped as to believe in a fundamental authority of what is merely sense-perception?" "What must be said, when Classical poetry, song, and other great arts, have joined scientific discovery, in proving the contrary notion, efficiently, to have been the relatively supreme experimental authorities in such matters?" Mere blinded faith in sense-certainty can, therefore, then be relegated, fairly speaking, to cause worry among the monkeys.

There is no proper mystery about the sources of the general deception of today's populations respecting the issues which I have identified here.

The widespread repression of what were otherwise the native creative power of human beings, is to be recognized as a fruit of the existence of systems, such as, for example, the ancient Roman empire, which reign over populations by means of stupefying them into a relatively submissive state of brutality. On that account, we have reached a point in the history of mankind, at which we can no longer expect mankind's species to escape the general destruction—even extinction—of our human species, if the still-prevalent reign of the oligarchical principle of today's "greenies" is permitted to be continued.

We are presently confronted, on precisely that account, by our rising sensibility of a threat to continued human existence, the which is now represented by some million or more of asteroids, and also some great comets, which could spell extermination of the human species as a consequence. A dependency on mere sense-perception, under such conditions, can not be justified by a sane society.

What holds most of us back, on this account, is a certain fear of the myth of merely "popular opinion."

Among sane citizens suitably challenged on such accounts as this, the present commitment to the reduction of the planet's human population, means, if continued, a virtually assured extinction of the human species from this planet. The accelerating rate of oncoming extinction-impulses, as even from the present "greenies" alone, is touching the perimeters of a threatened more general extinction. This suicidal quality of such a "green" impulse, is to be found in large regions of the planet this far. If it were not reversed, and that soon, an extinction-experience were becoming likely now; it is only the rate of such a catastrophe which waits to become known. Indeed, a rapidly growing portion of what pretend to be scientists gone-green, is committed to what is effectively mass-murder, whether or not they wish to participate in the oncoming flood of a global "green death." That is already currently in accelerating progress under the impulses supplied by such means as the mass-murderous measures expressed by the characteristics of that British imperial, monetarist system which has been already shown to be working its way toward a general genocide presently.

The Relevant Disease

Any decently informed experience with a retrospective view of mankind's known history, suffices to demonstrate that there is no threat from alleged "overpopulation" as such, which threatens mankind. A view but a generation or two ahead, promises the feasibility of reaching out from our Moon to Mars, and other places, by means of an appropriate development of thermonuclear-fusion technologies. In the meantime, the threats of mass-killing of the populations of the respective nations are actually prompted chiefly by the increasingly active promotion of the "green genocide" itself.

This is not exactly a matter of recent news in this matter. Mankind, within the span of merely several millions of years (or less) of generations of mankind, has increased the energy-flux density of the power of man to exist and prosper. Most of the delay in progress along those lines has been the product of the role of the oligarchical tyrannies which have been known since the Homeric account of the mass-murder of the population of Troy, and most probably much earlier.

On the other side of the limitations in view, we must include the fact that the Sun is to be expected to destroy itself within a billion years, or two. Human progress in science should be enabled to meet such a challenge, if we insist on such a distant perspective (and its implications along the way). Mankind does have a promising destiny within this universe, provided we create the progress. However, that happy thought depends upon eradicating the monstrously deadly threat of extinction, already beginning now. Such a mandate as that, is already located in the evidence of the development of the creative (e.g., "noëtic") powers of the human mind, the human mind which stands outside the bounds inhering in the animal kingdom.

The clearly evident likelihood of a relatively early extinction of the human species, lies entirely within our willful toleration of the degenerative tendencies inhering in the tradition of the oligarchical principle which has ranged, typically, from the Roman empire through the currently mass-murderous, extinction-inclined characteristics of the British empire and its Saudi companion which have been exhibited in their behavior in the original "9-11" crimes of September 2001, and the echo of that shown by President Barack Obama and his Saudi-linked accomplices in 2012.

This situation demands a counter-paradigm of global trends in human cultures, a true launching of new leaps in fundamental expressions of scientific progress set into motion by the true patriots of the human species today.

There is now more to be said on this account.

III. The Role of a Secret Science

In the opening chapter of this report, I had emphasized what might be considered as the "secret" principles of an actually modern, physical science. That means, in practice, leaving the department of blind faith in sense-perception as such.

Case in point:

Sense-perception as a practice of human individuals, is a childish sort of delusion. Since we humans, especially those from a modern sort of leading physical-science progress, should have reached the stage of intellectual development at which they had departed from blind faith in sense-perception as such, why should really intelligent workers in the fields of science continue to believe that sense-perception provides, in and of itself, actually direct insight into the ruling principles of the universe generally? Is it merely sense-perception which defines, and reigns over that universe in which many poorly informed, very credulous folk still believe: that the universe is run by the rules attributed to mere human sense-perception? What has the galaxy to testify about such matters as that? Sense-perception is undoubtedly useful for monkeys, but are we merely monkeys?

We represent actually noëtic capabilities which no species of mere beast replicates. Therefore, no variety of human being should have ever believed that mankind's species is delimited by the same rules as monkeys, or, in the alternative, those subjected to the brutish effects inherent in slavery, or to the particular kind of bestiality expressed by a brutish oligarchy such as that which mass-murdered Troy, or the victims of the Roman imperial arena. Since we know, that the human species is naturally possessed of synthetic qualities of specifically noëtic creative powers, as no mere animal has, why should mankind play according to the animal rules imposed on slaves, or by otherwise brutish types?

Return to the subject of our first chapter here: the secret of the human mind. The specific distinction of the human species from all others presently known to us, is the ability to experience the future, that precisely as Johann Sebastian Bach set the pace for all truly modern artistic composition, as the method to express

Bach, in his Preludes and Fugues, established the method by which all Classical artistic composition expresses the knowable future, the "specifically human potentiality which underlies all human discoveries of universal physical principles."

the knowable future, as Bach does that, repeatedly, in his **Preludes and Fugues**. That is the same specifically human potentiality which underlies all human discoveries of universal physical principles, and my own rather unique specific, if circumscribed talent of foreseeing the future of an economy even, sometimes, years in advance, as I had done at times. We who act so are not merely foreseeing the future; we are also equipped to create it. Therefore, we speak of a knowable future, a habit which is the essence of all human creativity, and our principled distinction from beasts, and also from those who insist on behaving as if they were merely beasts.

Such are the secrets now available to the willing human mind.

www.ingramcontent.com/pod-product-compliance
Lightning Source LLC
Chambersburg PA
CBHW080243260726
48658CB00008B/3211